Brighouse
in old picture postcards

by Pete Tiler

European Library

ZALTBOMMEL/THE NETHERLANDS

GB ISBN 90 288 4554 2

Second edition, 1997: reprint of the original edition of 1987.

INTRODUCTION

The subject of this book of old picture postcards and photographs, is the district covered by, and associated with, the Borough of Brighouse, as it was formed in 1893, until the outbreak of the Second World War.
Brighouse is a small industrious town in the Calder valley between the city of Bradford and the town of Huddersfield. Most small communal areas, that later sprang up to be towns and cities, can claim to be richer than Brighouse, having played a greater, more superficially conspicuous part in the history of England. Brighouse can claim no really famous national figures that were born in the area; no famous battles were fought on Brighouse soil. Brighouse has no historical buildings to speak of, but in its streets can be traced the development of the industrial greatness on which England was built.
As a town, Brighouse was a late starter, the total population of the whole area around 1750 being between three and four thousand. Most of the inhabitants lived on the surrounding hills at Southowram, Rastrick, Clifton and Hipperholme, only 370 living in Brighouse proper. So from a thinly populated area, when the industrial revolution began, we can plot the sudden growth of the housing and industrial buildings of the town, through the age of the steam engine and the canalisation of the Calder valley, up to the formation of the Borough of Brighouse and its eventual domination of the area.
The main problem is where to start our topic, but let us first explain the name Brighouse and how it came about. The name probably first appeared when a wooden bridge was built over the Calder river, where the Brighouse bridge now stands. When one or two houses were erected nearby, they became known as 'Bridgehouses'. So Brighouse is a corruption of 'bridge' and 'house'. Not being great enough to stand on its own, it became attached to a more populated neighbour and was called Hipperholme-cum-Brighouse.
At its inception the Brighouse area had its economic basis in wool production, its manufacture and trading, which expanded rapidly, clearing the forests in order to make sheep runs. James Armitage of Kirklees Hall held virtually all the land around the district, but hired it out to small-holders. Coal was worked in the Norwood Green area and cottage industries abounded. Quarries were mostly shallow affairs, because the stone had to be manhandled out by 'huggers', who wore saddles on their backs on which the stones were placed. In addition the carding and wire industries plus leather tanning were expanding.
The homes of the gentry were dotted all over the countryside; in Rastrick were the Boothroyd, Woodhouse, Thornhill and Toothill estates with the home of the Rastrick family-Lillands. In Hipperholme and Lightcliffe were Winteredge, Giles House, Hoile House; plus Rookes, Coley and Slead Halls, and in Brighouse; Hanson House was at Brighouse Park and of course Kirklees Hall, the aformentioned home of the Armitages.
The first step in the progress and prosperity of Brighouse came with the improvement of the roads. The only trouble arose from the setting up of tollbars along the turnpike roads. The Brighouse people, never slow to show their resentment at having to pay for something that had previously been free, rioted and in the revolt destroyed the tollbars at Bailiffe Bridge and Brighouse. Next came the

innovation of the Calder Navigation System, constructed by James Smeaton of Eddystone Lighthouse fame. With better forms of transport now moving through the valley, Brighouse began to develop more rapidly than its neighbours Hipperholme and Rastrick. New roads through the valley were built, including the Elland-Obelisk highway. Mills and mechanisation appeared and the steam age brought Watts steam engine to power the new machinery. Victoria Mills, Prince Albert and Britannia Mills of the woollen trade mingled with the dye-works at Brookfoot, the engineering Iron Foundry, and Woodhouse Iron and Brass Works. Collieries were in vigourous production and calico printing came to town introduced by William Robinson. The first newspapers were printed, banks and building societies were formed to help industry and property development.

One other mode of transport which brought people and goods to the town, was the Leeds-Manchester Railway Company, the section from Hebden Bridge to Normanton being laid between 1837 and 1840. The local station, built on the south side of the river Calder, was named the Brighouse and Bradford Station, as Bradford had no railway line at that time. Coaches met the passengers as they arrived and ferried them to Bradford or Huddersfield. A number of initial problems brought forth an article in 'Punch' magazine which read: *Their trains devided into three categories – those that arrived but did not start; those that started but did not arrive; and those that did neither*. But being able to transport goods to any part of the country by rail, gave a massive impetus to local industry. The postal system brought in orders from further and further afield.

As for local government, the area was still known as Hipperholme-cum-Brighouse until the formation of the Brighouse Local Board in 1895. By this time the main structure of Brighouse was laid out. Churches, schools and various societies sprang up in numerable quantity as the borough grew, taking under its umbrella Rastrick, Clifton and a large part of Southowram. Back to the fold came Hipperholme and Lightcliffe, at a later date; not as a big brother of Brighouse Borough Council, but as a junior partner.

Samuel Baines formed the first fire brigade in the town and bought a fire engine, in order to protect his property. Some firms maintained their own fire fighting force, even after the town had its own, at the Rydings, off Halifax Road.

The First World War came and went, and so too the years of unemployment. Quite a number of mills closed down or were converted into smaller light-engineering sites. The centre of the town gradually changed from houses to shops and banks, the housing moving to the outskirts. Now a very busy shopping centre, its face changing weekly as premises are demolished, altered and newly built, old Brighouse will live on in the memories of its senior citizens and in the pages of this book.

Acknowledgements:

Steven Firth of the Brighouse Echo for permission to reproduce photographs; Donald Waddington and Duncan Carter of the Collector's Club for helping to fill some gaps; and to Ralph Wade for helping me to identify some of the more obscure items.

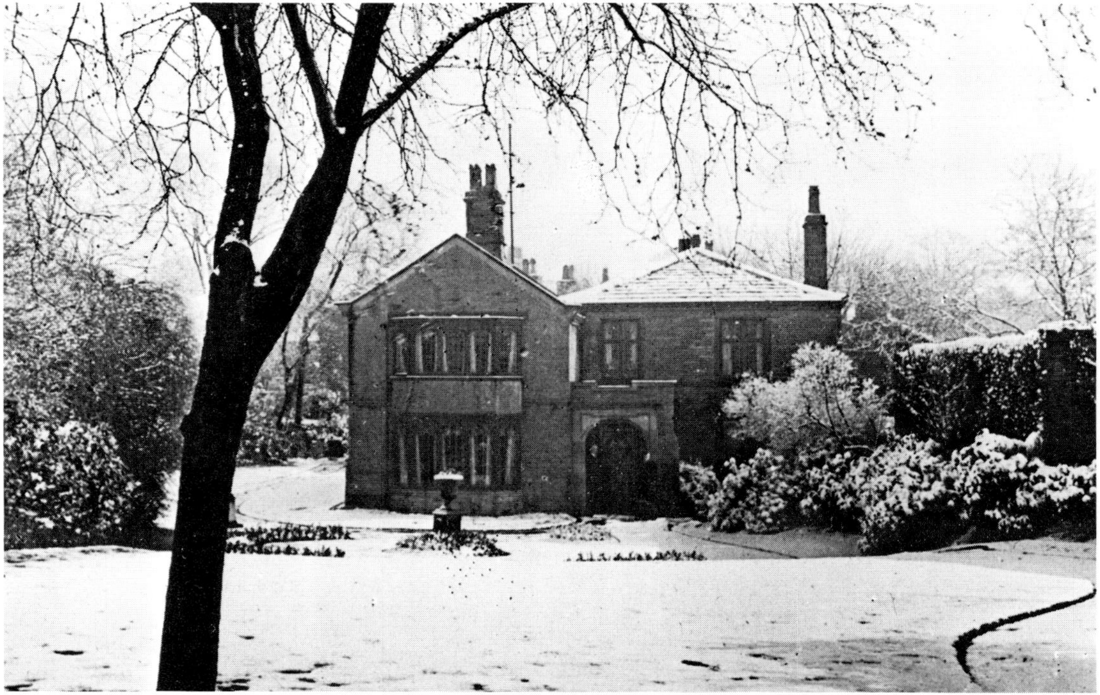

1. *Bonegate Hall.* This picture shows the front of Bonegate Hall, the ancestral home of the Brighouse family of Brighouse. It is situated just behind where the Ritz Ballroom now stands, at the junction of Bradford Road and Bonegate Road. The house is believed to have been built by Henry Brighouse in 1653, but the family name is much older, being mentioned in the court records of 1275. Bonegate means 'the street of the Bondsman', a bondsman being a person who held surety, and the land there was copyhold of the Manor Hall. The house passed to the Gill family in 1696 and by 1762 it was in the possession of the Ledgard family. Some of the outbuildings were demolished, after being left empty for a time, but the grounds where it stands have not been developed. The above picture was produced on part of a postcard entitled 'An April Snowstorm' circa 1908.

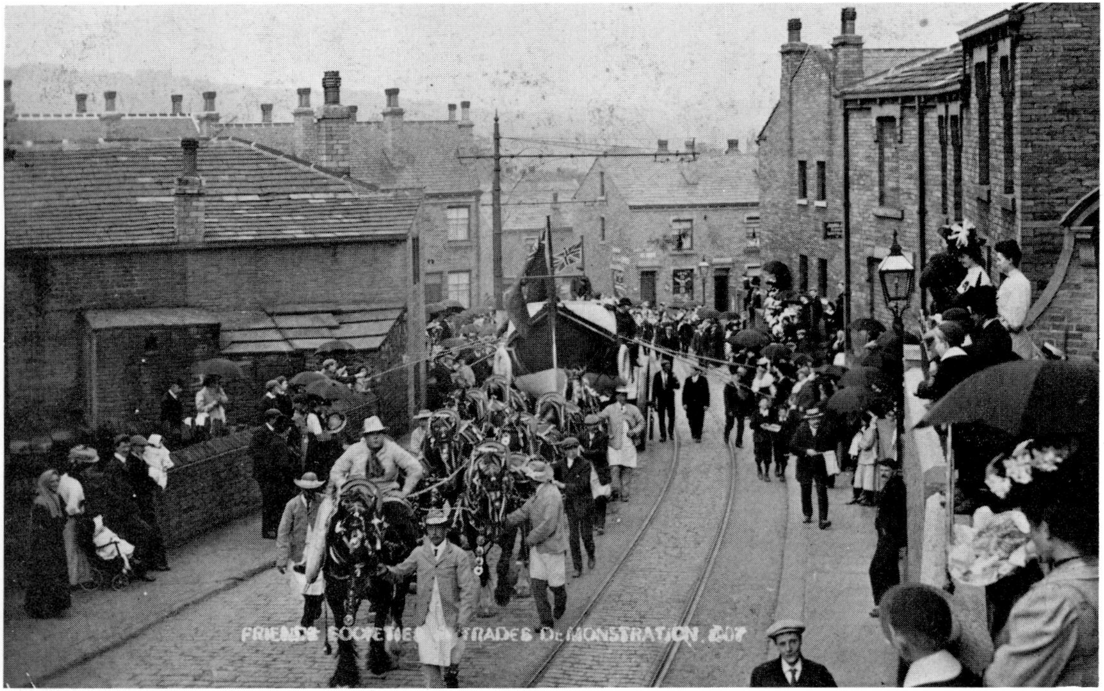

2. *Trade demonstration.* The proposed visit of Princess Louise, Duchess of Argyle, to open the new art gallery, sparked off the revival of the great parade of Friendly Societies and Trades Exhibition held on 22nd June 1907. Fifty-one traders took part, along with numerous societies. At least two fire brigades and quite a number of bands were on view as part of the exhibition which was held at Lane Head recreation ground. In fact, so much was arranged and the weather so unkind, that some of the events were held over until the following Saturday. This postcard shows the third section of the procession moving up Bonegate Road on the last leg of its journey. This section was sponsored by T. Sugden & Sons of Brighouse Flour Mills and shows Tom Castle, the fat boy sat astride the leading horse of nine, that were pulling a lifeboat, formally stationed at Worthing.

3. *Tom Castle.* The young man mentioned on the opposite page, Mr. Tom Castle, is possibly Brighouses best known fat boy. He was used on many advertisements as a mascot, by the local flour producing company of Thos. Sugden & Sons Limited, for quite a number of years. His hefty good health was supposed to have been brought about by his having eaten the products that had been made with Sugdens flour. Poor Tom, who just got fatter and fatter, died at the age of thirty years. As the picture postcard states, he weighed fifteen stones by the time he had reached his fifteenth birthday.

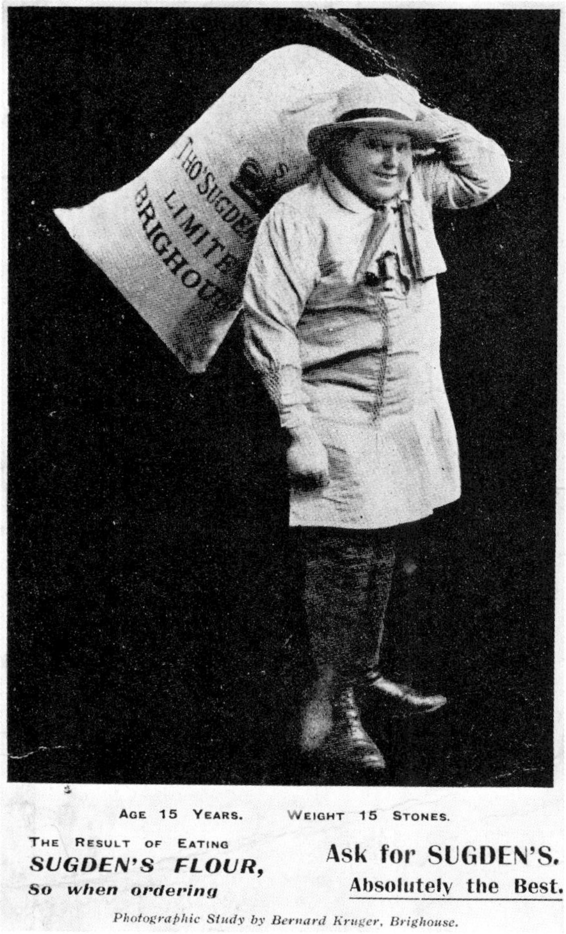

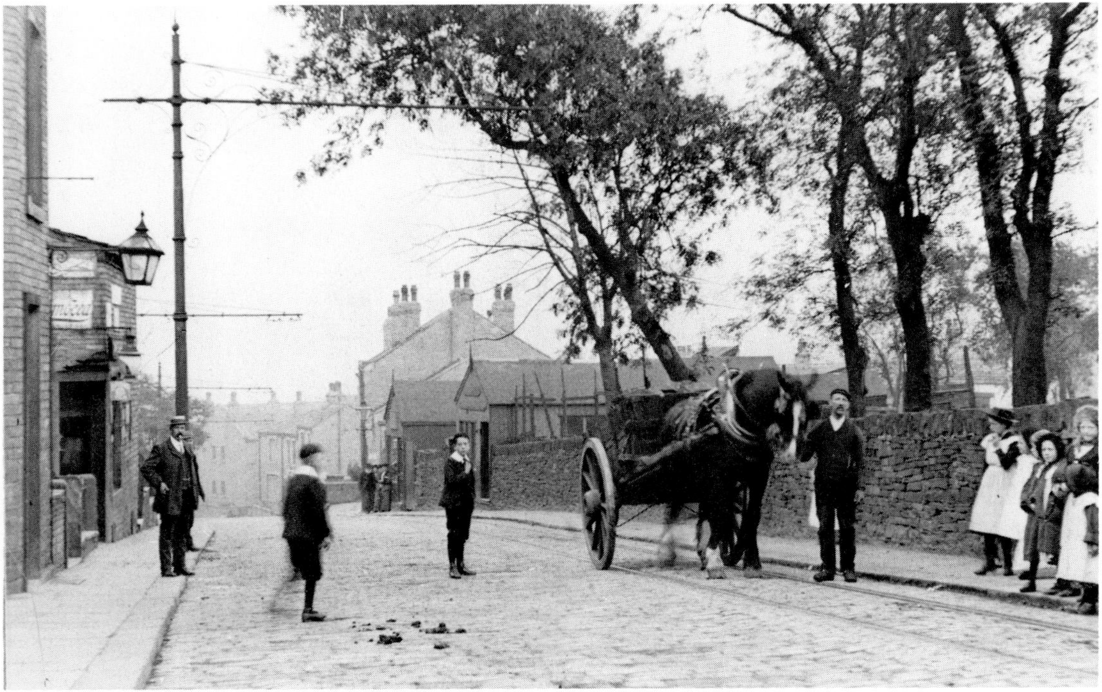

4. *Top of Bonegate.* About three hundred yards further up Bonegate Road, halfway between Church Lane and Waterloo Road, is where this photograph was taken. The building to the extreme left which included a barber's shop, has now gone, as have all the trees on the right side. Just in front of the moving boy in the picture is the opening to Church Lane; now a double-fronted shop stands at the farther corner. The large house and the two wooden huts on the top side of Church Lane have long since disappeared and have been replaced by the Churchfield Hall, residence for the Plymouth Brethren and a row of new houses, built where those beautiful trees once stood.

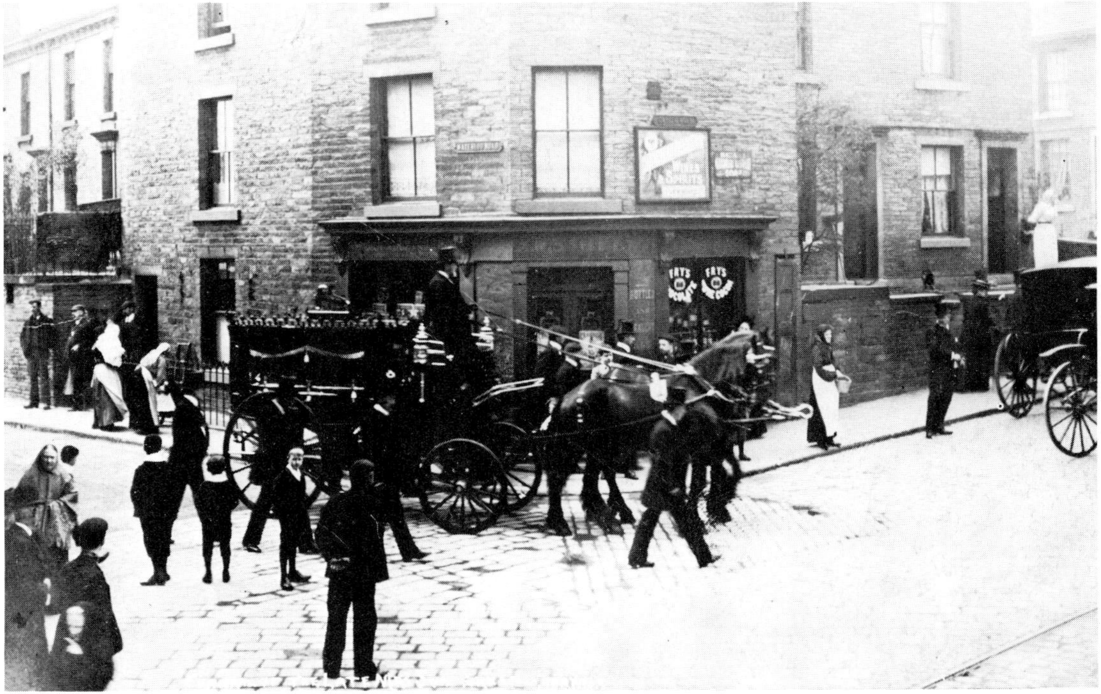

5. *Funeral procession.* On the corner of Bonegate Road and Waterloo Road we capture an incident that happened on 10th May 1905. The funeral procession of Mrs. Susan Sunderland, the 'Yorkshire Queen of Song', who died on 7th May, was making its way to the Brighouse cemetary on Lightcliffe Road. She was born on 30th April 1819, the daughter of Mr. and Mrs. J. Sykes of Spring Gardens, a farm near where Lightcliffe Road crosses Garden Road. Mrs. Sunderland held major concerts in London and in 1860, her light soprano voice was heard at Buckingham Palace by Queen Victoria. She retired in 1864 to give music lessons and later started a subscription fund for song competitions which are still held nowadays at Huddersfield Town Hall. Luke Settle, a local blacksmith, started here with singing lessons, beating time for her on his anvil. The shop you can see in the picture is now Dots Cozy Corner Café.

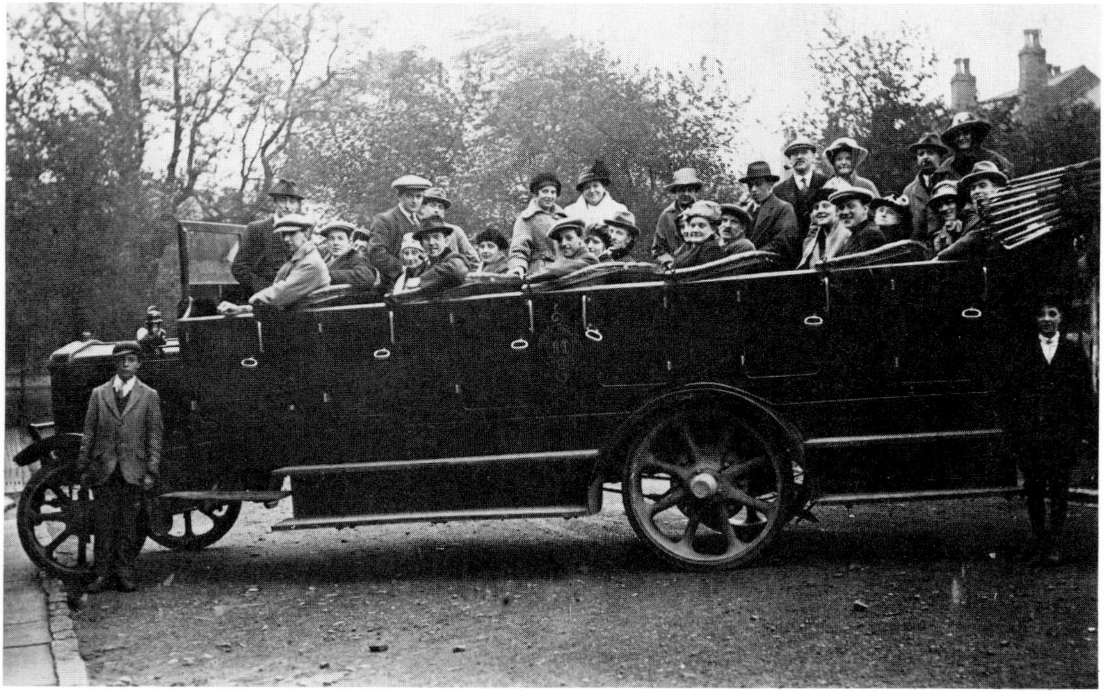

6. *Outing*. The residents of Kimberley Street, off Bonegate Road, are pictured here about to take a char-à-banc outing, circa 1912. This solid tyre motor vehicle, with runner boards and acetylene lamps, would have been used as a wagon for most of the week and for coach trips at weekends. A number of individuals in Brighouse had such char-à-bancs; Davison Brothers and J.P. Nelson of Briggate were two such business' that used to ply for hire in Thornton Square around 1920. Percy Garside, who later became a concert party star, would have been able to remember his father having a similar vehicle. Some of the people to be recognised on board are: Florence and Lawrence Saunders, Mr. and Mrs. A. Crabtree and Mr. and Mrs. William Bottomley.

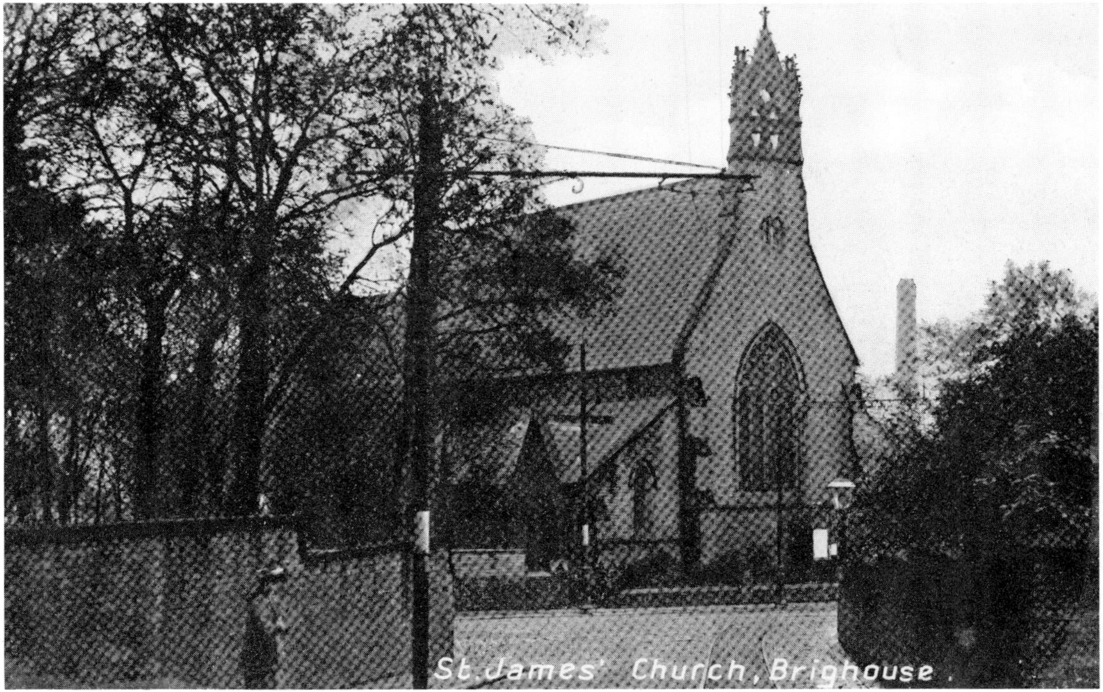

7. *St. James' Church.* On the opposite side of Bradford Road from Bonegate Hall stood St. James' Church, complete with bell-tower. The Church of England tried for many years to set up a mission church in the old St. Paul's Chapel but failed. The idea to establish a foothold in the centre of Brighouse remained however, and in 1867 an appeal for the building of a new church raised £1,427 to purchase land from Mrs. Camm, in the south corner of Wellholme Park. By April 1870 the church was built; an organ was installed and in July 1871 the two stained-glass windows, made by Morris & Co. of Bloomsbury were added. The total cost of the structure was between £3,000 and £4,000. Just over one hundred years later the building was demolished.

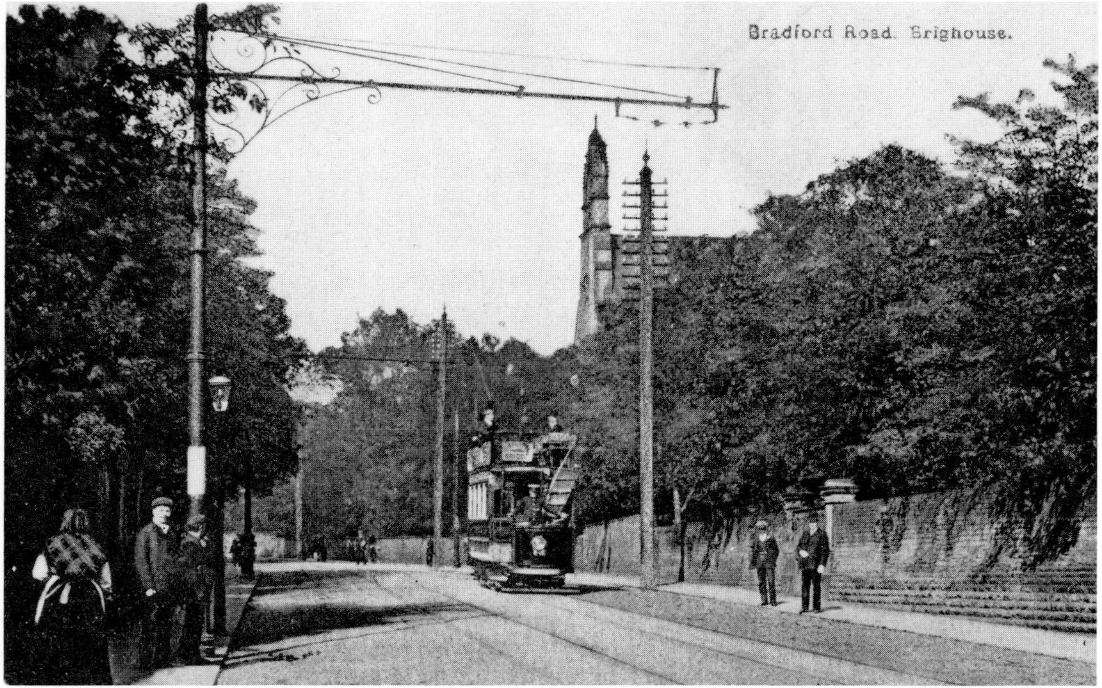

8. *Bradford Road.* From St. James' Church we move closer to the town centre, but cast a glance back along Bradford Road. In the centre of the postcard we note the tram proceeding towards Brighouse on the Bailiffe Bridge track. The other track is the Halifax line that turned left into Bonegate Road just beyond St. James' Church. On the left, in place of the trees, you would now find the Ritz Ballroom. It was initially built as the Ritz Cinema, later it was opened as a night club called the Stardust Showbar, before being converted into a ballroom. To the right-hand side the church and all the trees on that side of the picture are now gone and Bates' Garage would be seen in the distance. Welholme Park is in the far distance.

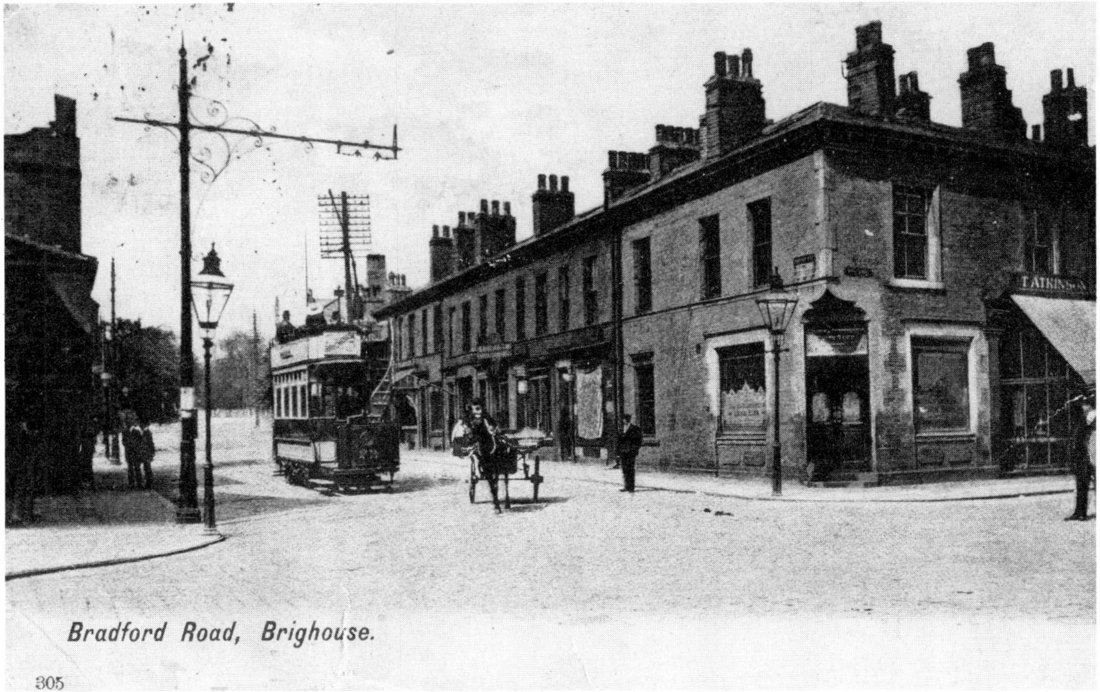

9. *Bradford Road, Brighouse.* The next view is of Brighouse town centre where Bradford Road, King Street, to the right, and Commercial Street, to the left, meet. This junction was the terminus for the Halifax trams that ran from Bailiffe Bridge and from Halifax town centre. The extension to the tramway reached Hipperholme in November 1902, it moved the terminus to the Dusty Miller at Hove Edge, in June the following year. At the beginning of March 1904 the first tram, driven by the Deputy Mayor of Brighouse, A.O. Stocks, reached the 'George Corner', so named because of the George Hotel, whose brewery can just be seen to the left in the picture. The Bailiffe Bridge line was opened in October of the same year. To the right of the picture, the building on the corner was the Halifax and Huddersfield Union Bank.

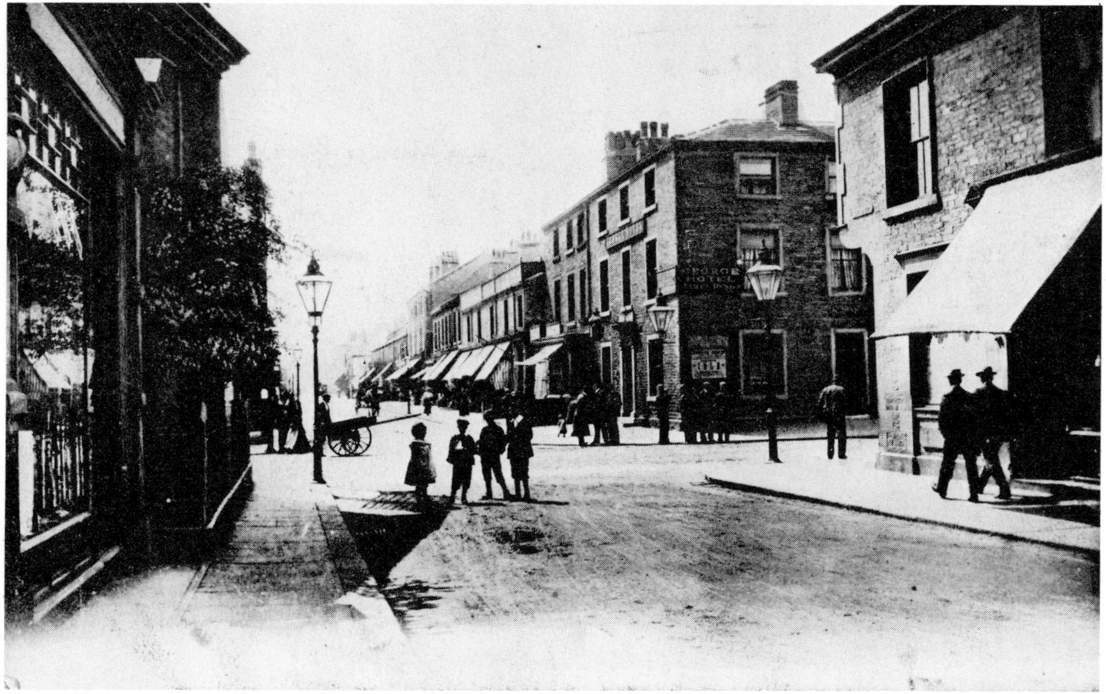

10. *Commercial Street.* At the beginning of 1906 the terminus of the Halifax tram was moved about thirty yards back along Bradford Road to outside the Oddfellows Hall, because the George Corner was becoming congested. The George Hotel, on the corner, as we look along Commercial Street, was owned from October 1874 by Henry Lockwood who succeeded a Mr. Hartley. At that time, as no German yeast was available for baking, brewers' yeast has to be used. This was obtained at either a public house, or from hawkers, who went about the streets, and delivered twice a week. David Wood supplied the George Hotel with yeast and called on many a housewife, who made bread and also brewed their own ale while their husbands were out at work. When Mr. Lockwood died, the contractor who built the Town Hall, James Dyson, took over the George Hotel on 22nd February 1889.

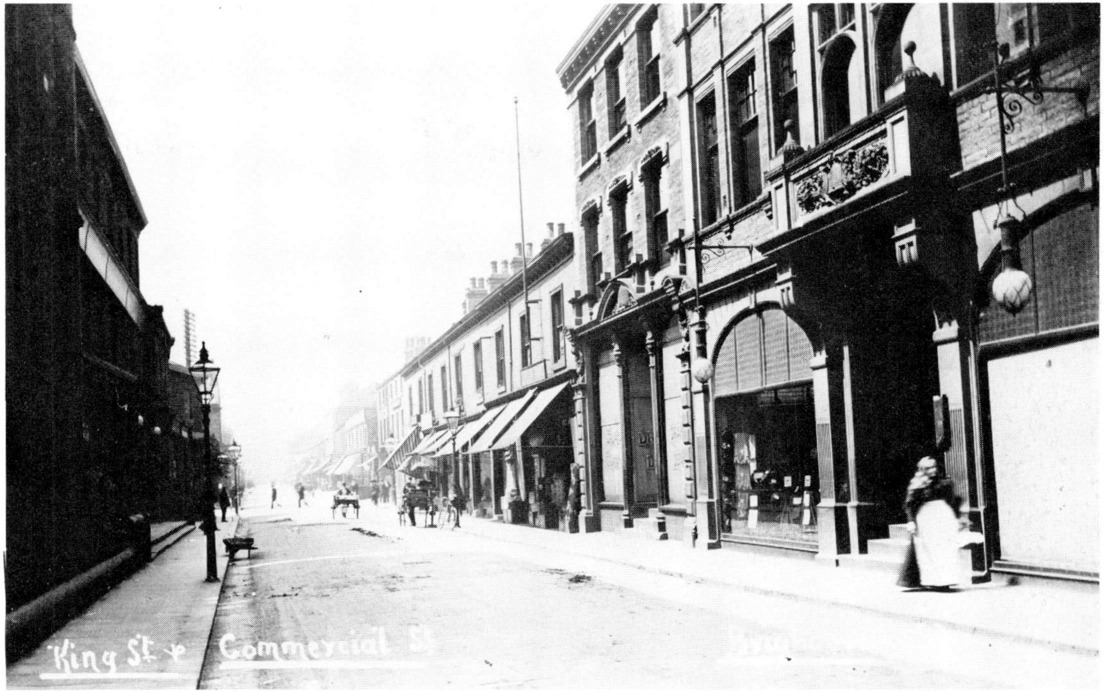

11. *King Street and Commercial Street.* This picture postcard is a view of King Street, from the Round House public house end. To the extreme left is the old, Grecial style St. Paul's chapel, opened on 27th October 1885, by the Wesleyan Methodists. Due to falling attendance, the building was sold and became a wireworks in 1949. When the wireworks closed, the premises were demolished and a car park laid out for the new Co-operative self-service store. The large building to the right was, and still is, the main section of the Brighouse Co-operative Society, built in 1864 at a cost of £2,000, but the frontage is very different today. The beautiful hanging global lamps have long ago disappeared, and a modern shop frontage has replaced the old.

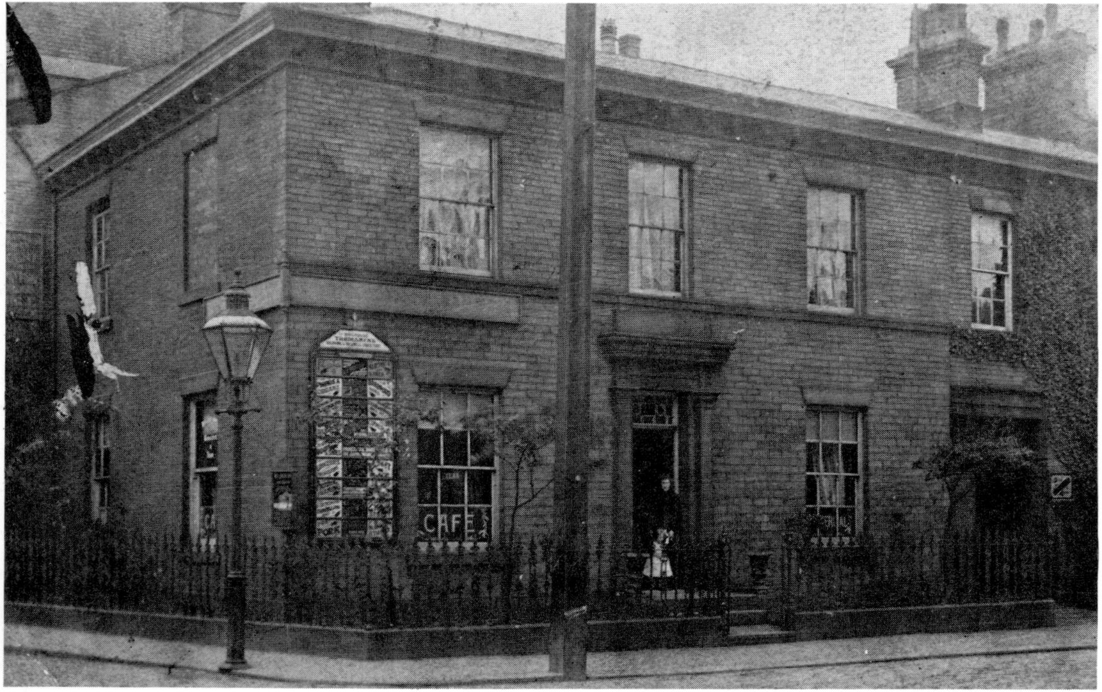

12. *Café.* Now we are back at the corner of King Street, diagonally opposite the George corner, and an area which changed dramatically in just a few short years. In 1906 it looked like this, with Parkers Café on the ground floor and a small hotel above. The large advertisement board, on the wall, by the lamp post reads: *Brighouse Tradesmans Shopping And Business Directory. E.E. Webster, Pawnbroker of 45, Bethel St. and 3, Park St. – Thorntons for pianos & organs, Bradford Rd. – J. Lawson, cycles and repairs, 68/70, Commercial St. – ? Smith, Tel.: No. 16 Commercial St. – George Mitchell, boots and shoes, Commercial St. – A. Kitson & Son, grocery provisions, Market Place – L. Watson, tobacconist/picture framing, 54, Bradford Rd. – E.M. Littlewood, 2, King St., stationery/travelling – T. Atkinson, King St. pork pies.*

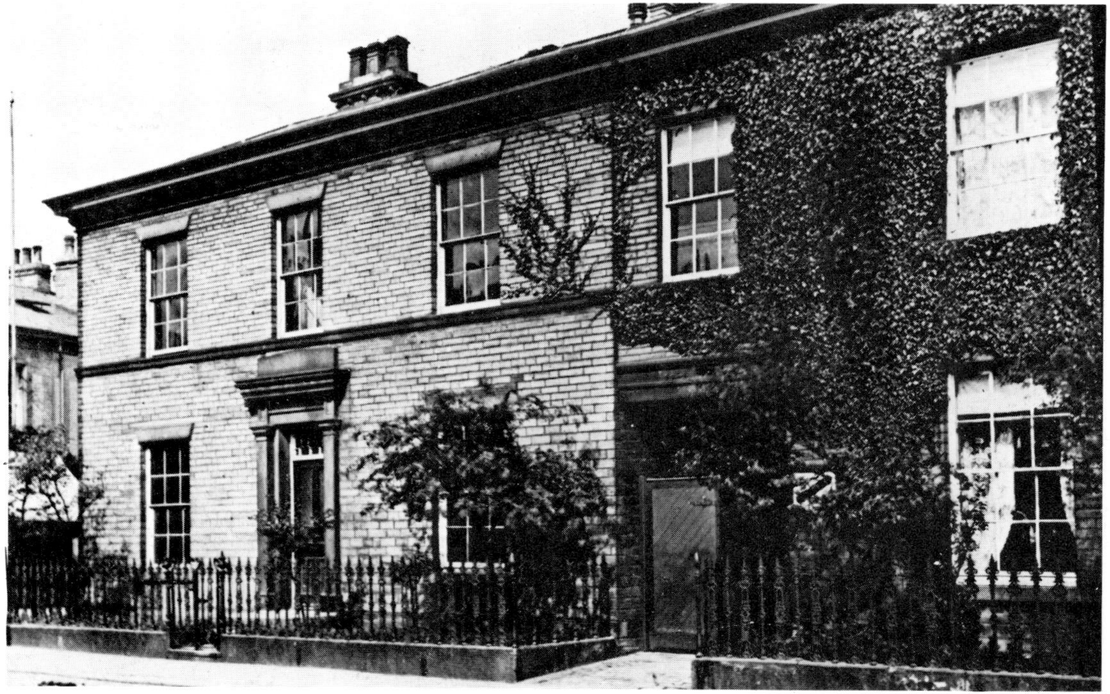

13. *First Change.* By 1910 this is how the corner looked; the Tradesmans Shopping and Business Directory advertisement board had disappeared. The café had closed its doors and the hotel sign boards had also gone. Next door, the house with ivy clinging all over it, has a small sign by the entrance almost covered by the ivy. This proves that doctor Brown was still in residence at 22, Bradford Road. Through the bushes at the extreme left is T. Atkinsons shop, with the flag-pole outside, which for some reason had been moved four shops nearer the main Bradford Road. A complete face-lift was given to the whole area some years later.

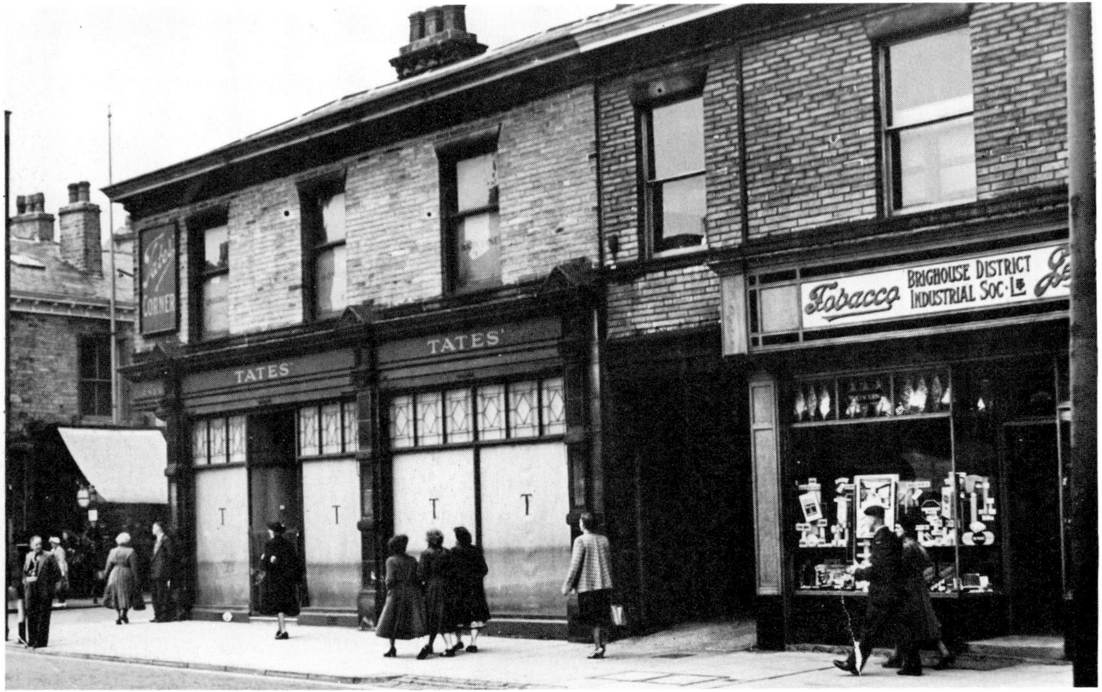

14. *Tate's Corner.* Around fifteen to twenty years later the area had a new name. The sign-board at the end of the building now reads 'Tates Corner' and it is still known as such today by most 'Briggus' folk. Tate's shop sold baby linen, hosiery and underwear according to the three upper windows. Even Doctor Browns house had been altered and the Brighouse District Industrial Society had built a tobacconists shop where Black Cat cigarettes could be purchased, including gift coupons, at ten for 9d. Tates was later taken over by the Brighouse Co-operative Society and is still owned by them, although it has altered, having been changed into a new supermarket which stretches the full length of King Street to the car park, where the wireworks once stood.

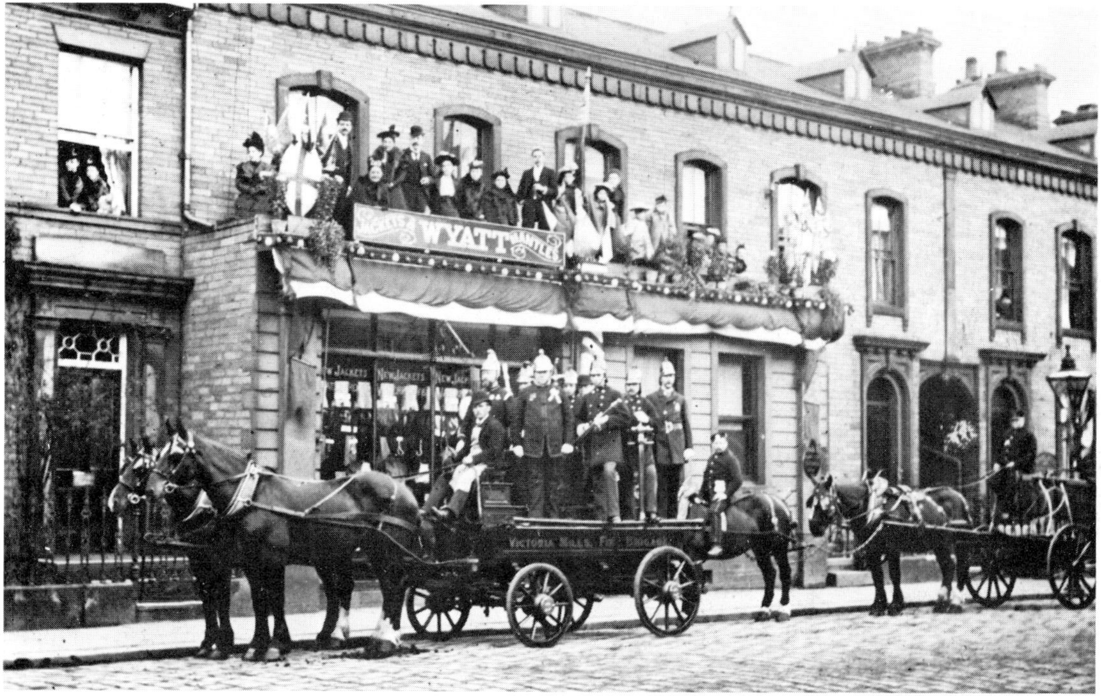

15. *Fire Brigade.* Next door to Doctor Browns house stood Wyatts clothiers, who sold jackets and a type of cloak called a mantle. In front of Wyatts shop is the Victoria Mills Fire Brigade, which was started in 1855 by Samuel Baines, when he acquired a fire engine and named it Neptune. He purchased the engine to protect his property the Victoria Mills, hence the name of the brigade, but eventually he was called to quite a number of other fires. When a disastrous fire burned down Sugden's flour mill in 1895 it was realised how inefficient Neptune was, as it could not pump enough pressure to shoot water to the top of the blazing building. In 1906 Neptune made her last journey from Victoria Mills to the scrapyard, but by this time Brighouse had its own fire brigade. The Yorkshire Bank now stands in the place of Wyatts shop.

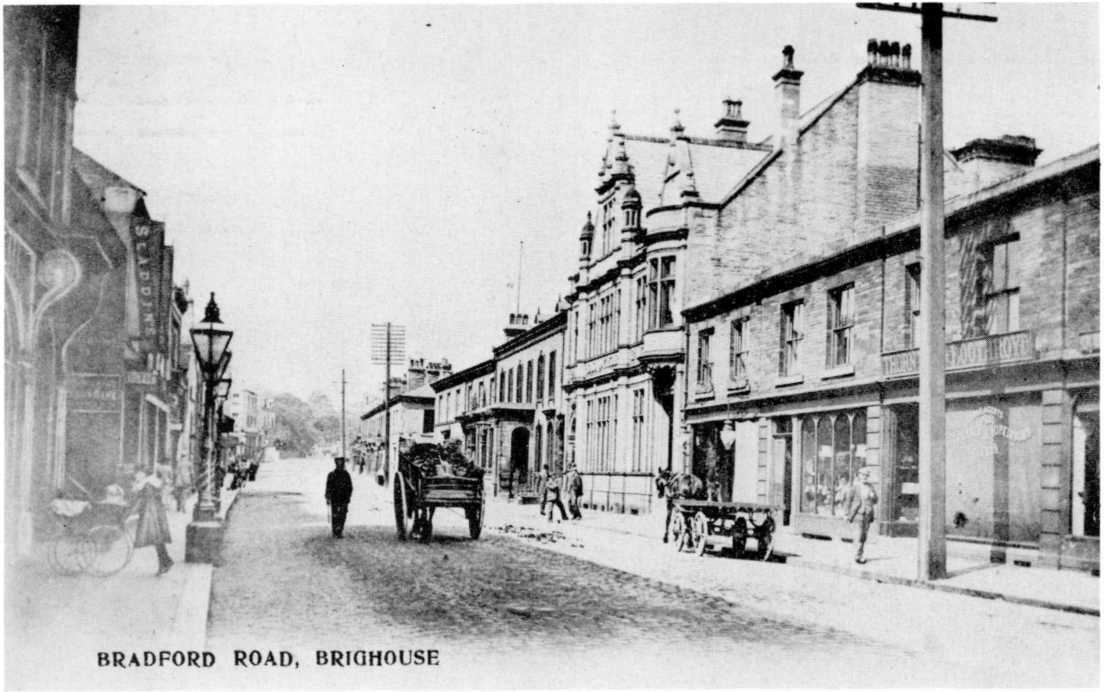

16. *Ball Flash.* Moving further along towards the end of Bradford Road, we can look back and see the magnificent building, built for the London and Yorkshire Bank Ltd. In later years it became the National Westminster Bank. Thornton and Boothroyds shop, far right, was the place to go for pianos and other musical items. The opposite side of Bradford Road was known as Ball Flash and in the mid-nineteenth century, one William Drake, who lived in the area, decided his chimney needed sweeping. Hoping to dislodge some of the soot and save himself money, he fired off his gun up the chimney. The result was that he set fire to his cottage chimney, and the joiners shop next door, belonging to Thomas Bottomley. Both premises were burnt to the ground, but no one was hurt.

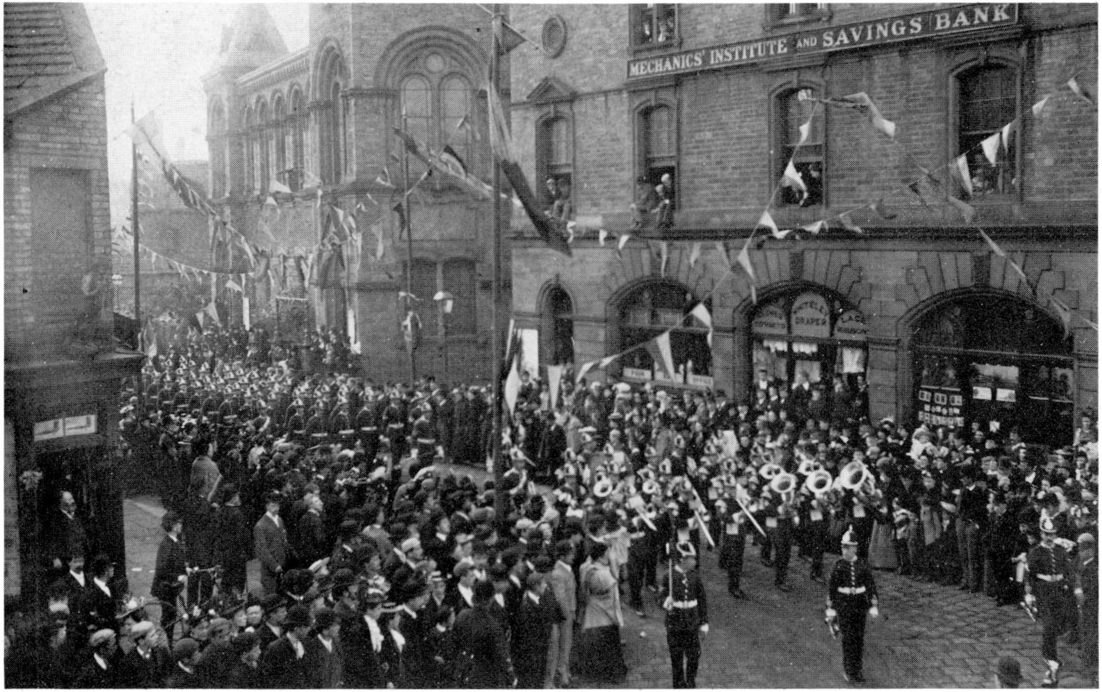

17. *Town Hall.* Where Bradford Road changes its name to Huddersfield Road, Bethel Street meets them from the west and this picture is taken looking into that street. The large building on the right was built as the Town Hall Buildings, which included the Town Hall on the corner, eight shops and a number of lecture rooms. As you can see in the photograph the Mechanics Institute, founded in 1846, moved its headquarters there when it was opened in 1868. The Institute was initially set up 'to instruct the members in the principals of the arts they practised and in the various branches of science and useful knowledge'. The Institute closed down in 1910 when the technical school it ran was taken over by the Government Schools. Nowadays the right-hand corner in the photograph is called 'Whiteleys Corner', but in those days Whiteleys drapery was on the opposite side of Bethel Street. Further along can be seen Park Methodist Church, which is now being altered to an indoor market.

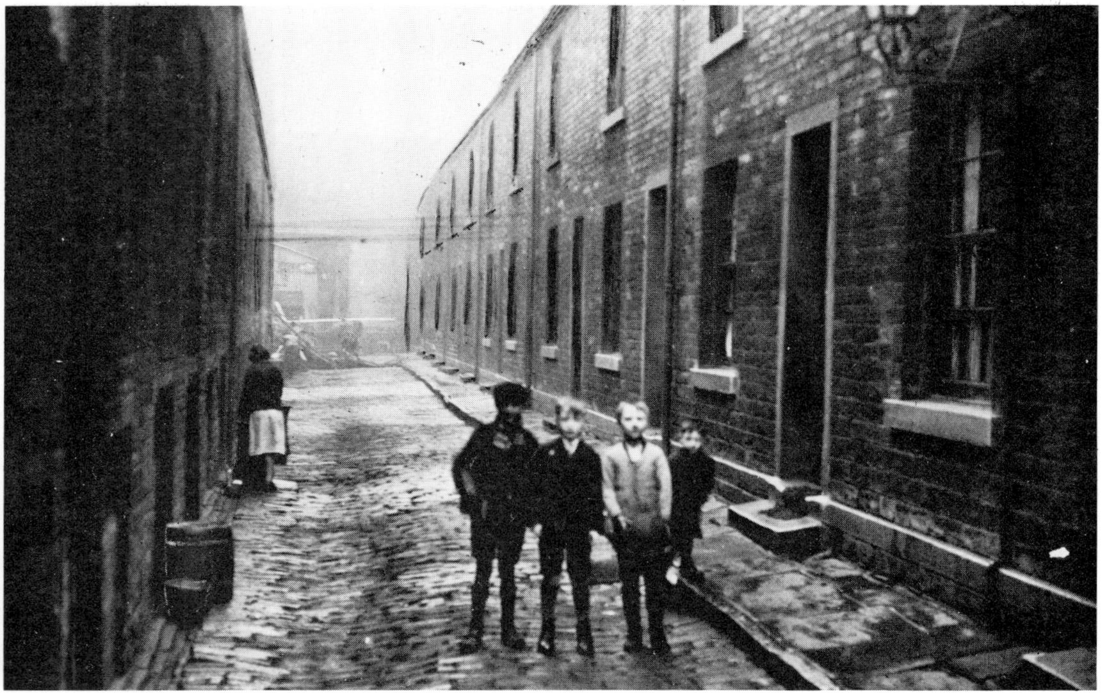

18. *Baines Row*. These young lads seem to be saying 'Would anyone like a game of footy', but where are they? On the opposite side of the junction of Bradford Road and Huddersfield Road, from Bethel Street, were Police Street and Mill Lane. The above scene is of a dingy little street, behind Mill Lane and close to Victoria Mill called Baines Row and is set around 1925. Nearly all of the slums in Brighouse disappeared during the second half of the boroughs existence due in part to a very progressive policy by the council members. This area was cleared fairly recently when the new Brighouse ring road was built. J.R. Gregson, the noted dramatist, was born, and lived for a number of years, not far from this row, in Mill Lane.

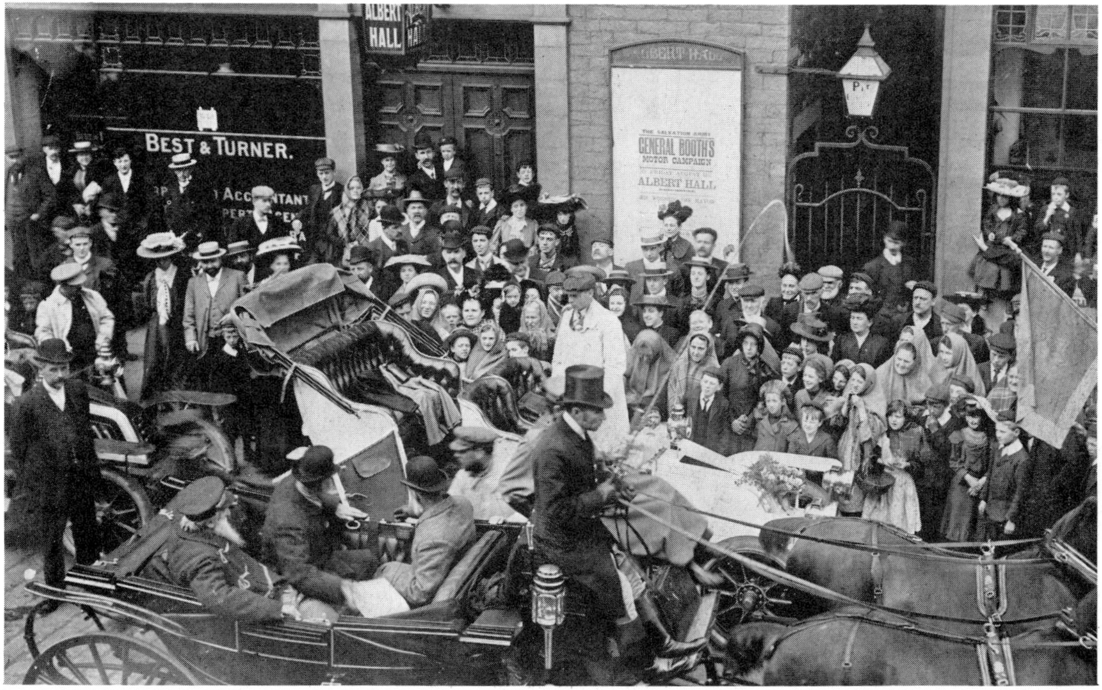

19. *William Booth.* The Reverend William Booth, General of the Salvation Army and Commander-in-Chief of all its subsiduary institutes, was awarded a civic welcome by Brighouse on his visit to the town, on 11th August 1905. He was born on 10th April 1828 and at fifteen he started to preach in the open air around Nottingham, as a Methodist and became a minister in 1852. He resided at Brighouse in 1857-1858 in a building that is now owned by Kirklees Printing on Bethel Street. He resigned his ministry in 1861 and travelled to London where, after some years of evangelical work, he started the Salvation Army in 1878. A branch of the S.A. was formed in Brighouse in 1887 and the Mission is now across the street from where General Booth used to reside. On his visit, a public meeting was held at the Albert Hall, a place of stage shows; later a cinema, and now a bingo hall. The religious group that he formed was to be called the Voluntary Army, but Booth substituted the word 'Salvation'.

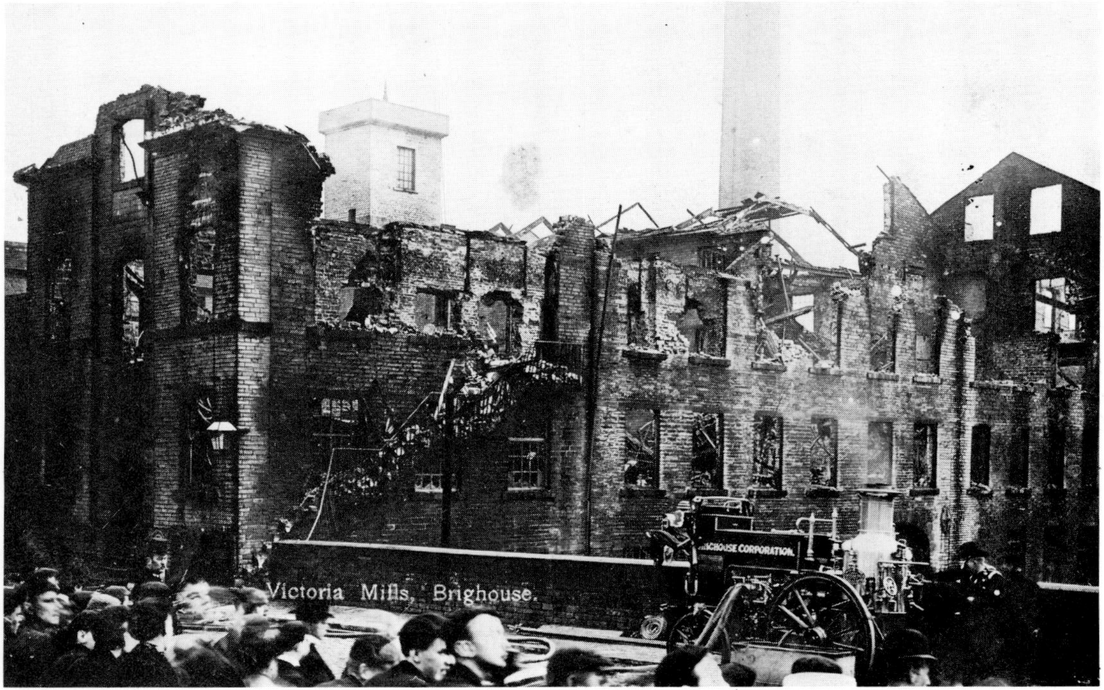

20. *Victoria Mills*. The Victoria Mills, situated behind Mill Lane and further along Huddersfield Road, was built by J. and H. Noble in 1837 and was used by a silk waste dressing firm. Later it was bought by Samuel Baines, along with Prince Albert Mill, the Canal Mill and various pieces of property along Bradford Road. Samuel Baines died in 1866 and the property was then being used as a cotting spinning mill by J. and H. Stott, employing about one hundred and fifty hands. Being built alongside the canal and within a couple of hundred yards of the railway station, it was in an ideal spot for sending goods by either mode of transport. But when a fire took place in 1905, although the mill had its own fire brigade, the fire engine was on its last 'legs', and could not save the mill from being gutted.

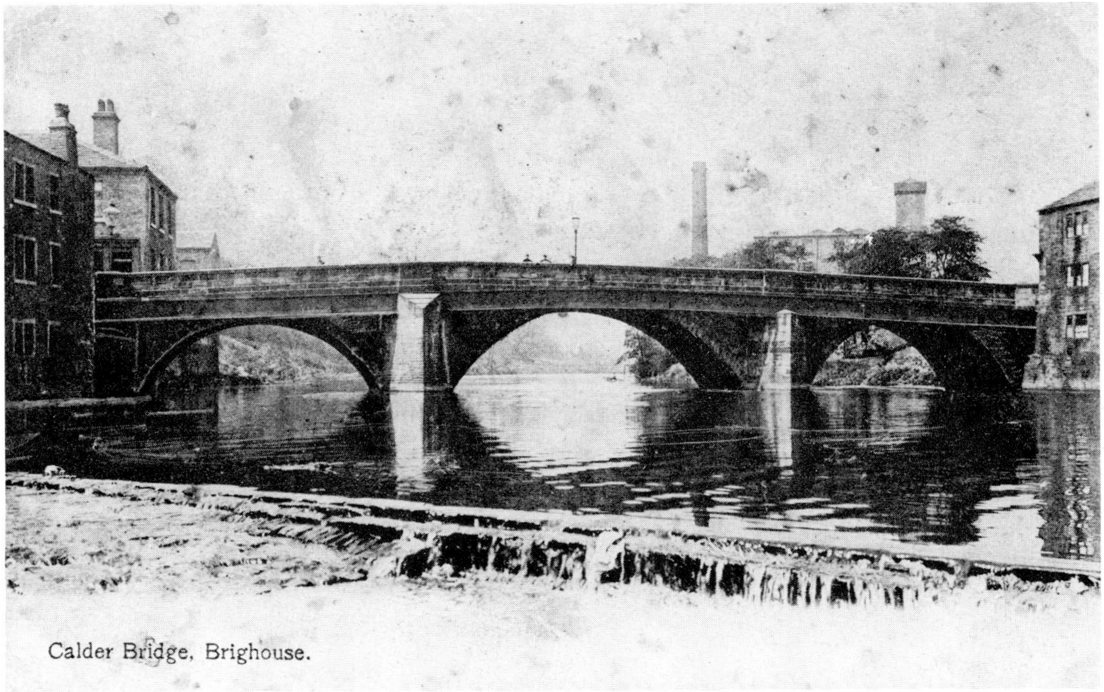

21. *Calder Bridge.* Moving from the canal bridge towards Huddersfield we would next cross the Calder Bridge or Brighouse Bridge as it is known. Up to 1824 Brighouse had only one bridge spanning the river Calder; that was at Bridge end and it was built in 1275. In 1824 the Bradford-Huddersfield turnpike road was constructed, one carriageway wide, bridging the Calder close to an old ford crossing, which had existed there from before Roman times. The remains of this can still be seen, passing through the water to the left of the bridge. In 1875 the tolls on the turnpike roads were abolished and the bridge was widened in 1905. In 1923 the Huddersfield Corporation laid tram-lines over the bridge from Huddersfield town centre to Tates Corner, Bradford Road. The last tram to run was in 1940, from when the trolley-bus took over the route.

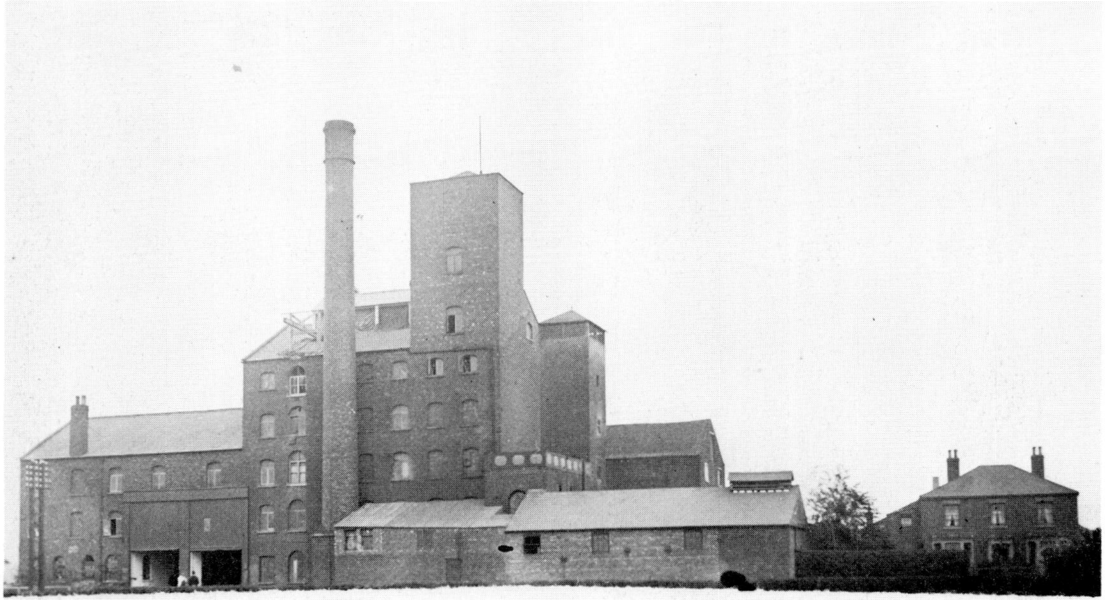

22. *Sugden's Flour Mill.* In 1832 Thomas Sugden, deciding to expand from his grocery business, built the Perseverence Mills, and thus established the myth that there has always been a flour mill in the centre of Brighouse. When Mr. Thomas R. Sutcliffe retired from work, he put up for sale the Old Brighouse Mill, which was bought by the Sugdens, rebuilt and enlarged. Shortly after the Brooks Corn Mill alongside, was added to the site. Old Brighouse Mill was built about halfway between Brighouse Bridge and Rastrick Bridge and has stayed under the ownership of the Sugden family from that time onward. The Sugdens have been active participants in Brighouse, both in industry and in politics. It was one Henry Sugden who stood up in front of the rebellious crowds outside the Town Hall, trying to calm them, at the time of the Irish riots. He was also the first county councillor for Brighouse and Rastrick, on the formation of the West Riding County Council.

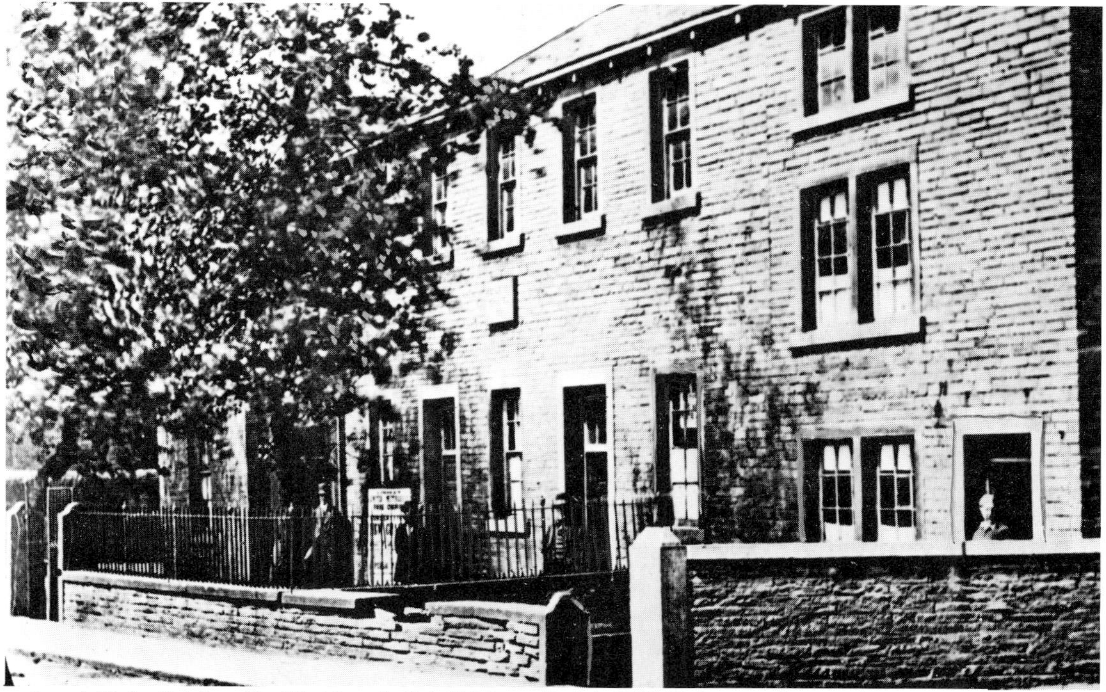

23. *New Connection.* A Methodist chapel had first been built in Brighouse Park in 1795. Unfortunately around that time there came a split in the ranks, with the Wesleyans under John Sharps direction coming into being and the New Connection taking over Park Chapel. After a law suit against the New Connection Methodists, the Wesleyans won possession of Park, and the New Connection quickly adjusting themselves to the situation, built the above chapel only a number of yards further along Bethel Street from where Park Chapel stood. In 1849 another rift, over the church government, produced a branch called the United Methodists who retained Park, the Wesleyans moving into the old Bridge end Chapel. This photograph was taken in 1896 after some of the rifts had been mended and the board outside the chapel is headed United Methodists, although the amalgamation of all factions did not take place until 1905, just before this building was demolished, making way for the building now owned by Kirklees Printing.

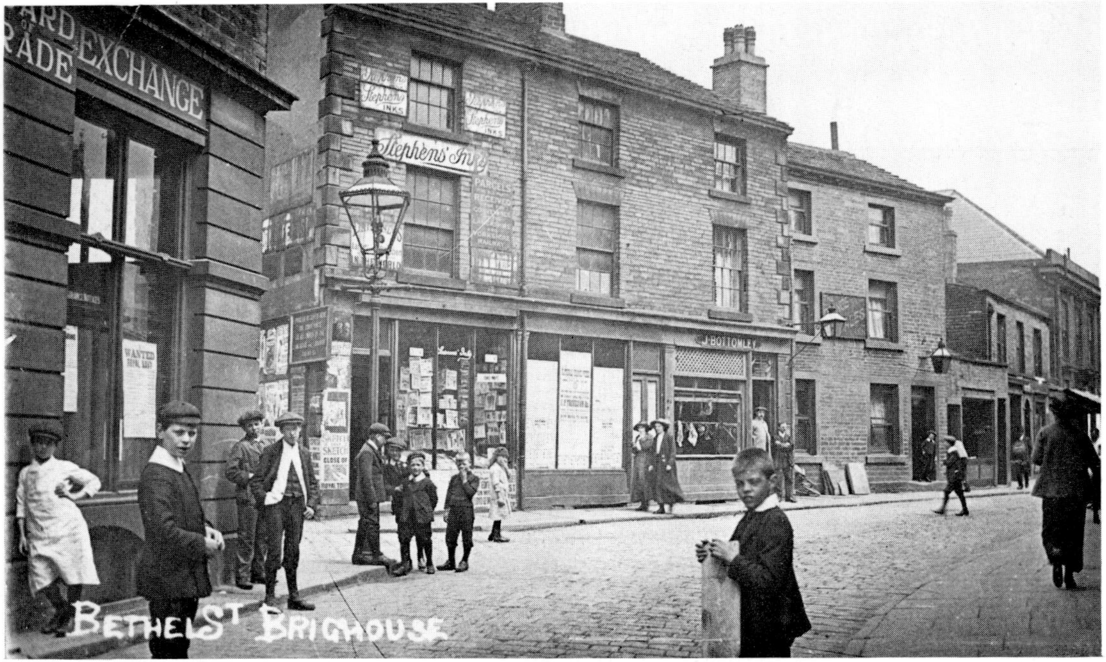

24. *Bethel Street.* The above picture postcard shows a scene, looking along Bethel Street, from the Briggate end, circa 1910. Holroyd Buildings also known as the triangle, is on the extreme left of the picture. Part of this building, at that time housed the Board of Trade and Labour Exchange, the entrance to which was around the corner by the gas lamp and was directly opposite the municipal buildings, which later became the Town Hall. Holroyd Buildings were demolished in 1913 to make room for Thornton Square, named after the then Mayor Robert Thornton. The shop behind the gas lamp advertises: 'Parcels for all parts received here for conveyance by the Lancashire and Yorkshire Railway'. This was Jonas Foxs newsagents shop and next door but one, the butchers shop belonged to J. Bottomley who did his own slaughtering. The Prince of Wales public house, with the wheelbarrow and flagstones leaning against its wall, looks rather bare without its mock Tudor frontage of today. The Prince of Wales was rebuilt in 1926 with timber from H.M.S. Donegal, a wood-built battleship launched in 1858.

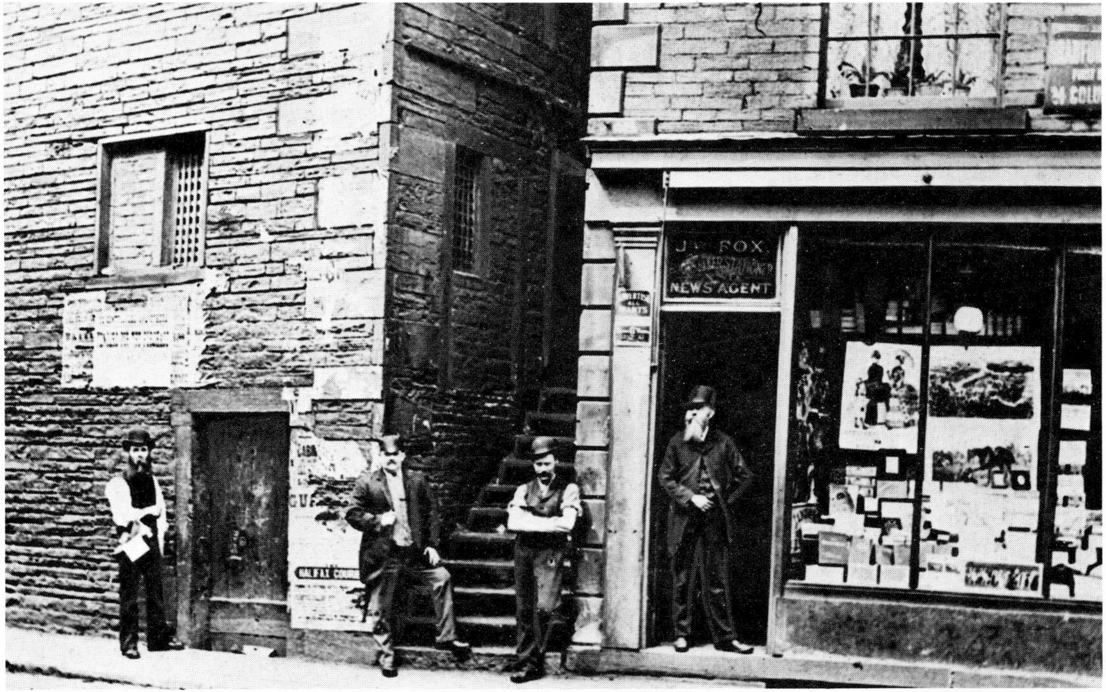

25. *Jonas Fox.* A little earlier than the previous picture is this photograph of Jonas Fox's shop. The engraved glass sign over his door states that he was a bookseller, stationer and newsagent and the smaller sign to the left of the shop door reads: 'Advertise all wants at 6d. weekly.' You will notice that most of his enamel signs had not been erected at this time. Over to the left of the picture, standing in front of the old malt kiln, we see a gentleman who was to become Mayor of Brighouse in 1919, David Crowther Holmes, a staunch Methodist, a magistrate and liberal party president, was the only member on the 1893 Borough Council who had not been Mayor. His mayoral roll did not last long however, as he became ill and died in 1920. The building he is standing in front of made way for Market Street and the municipal buildings.

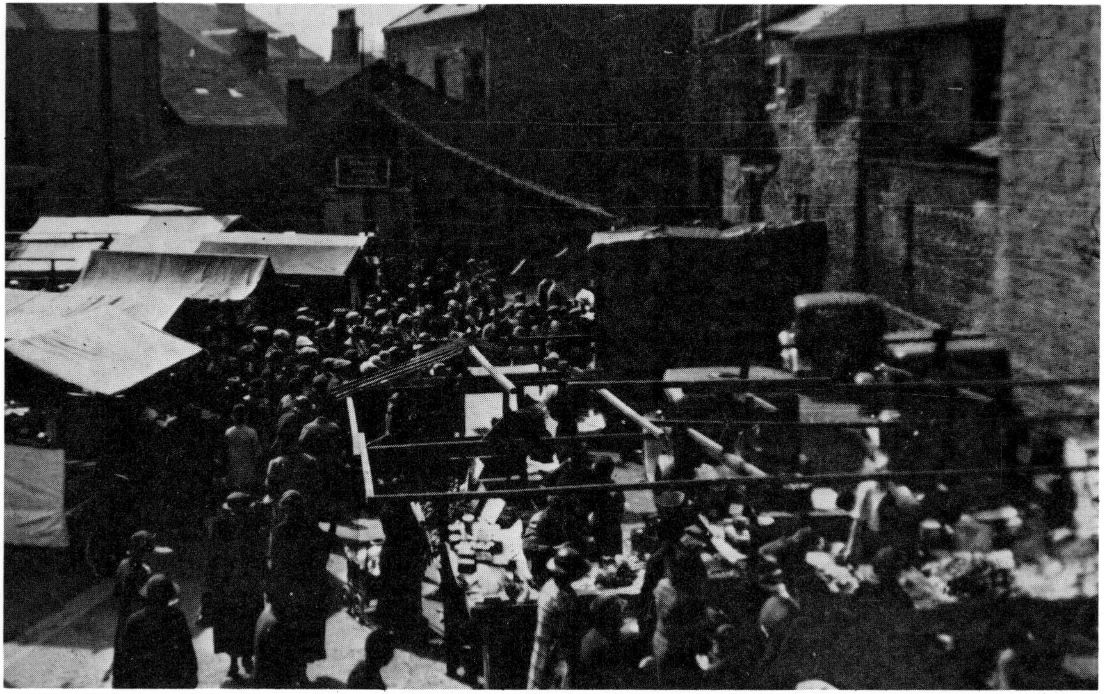

26. *Borough Market.* When Market Street was first opened, it was so named because the Borough Market had been situated between the municipal buildings and the back of the Ring O' Bells public house, and shops that fronted onto Commercial Street. Market Street linked Bethel Street and Commercial Street and gave access to the market. At this time the town had two open air markets; this one and the King Street Market which was at the top of Police Street near the junction with King Street. The Borough Market in the picture above moved, firstly behind Commercial Street, off Hutchinson Lane, when Gooder Street and Oxford Street were demolished, and then to where it is now beside the canal. The first bus station was built on the above site and then later followed the Borough Market to its present site behind Commercial Street. Now of course the above area is covered by the new shopping precinct and everyone of the above buildings have disappeared.

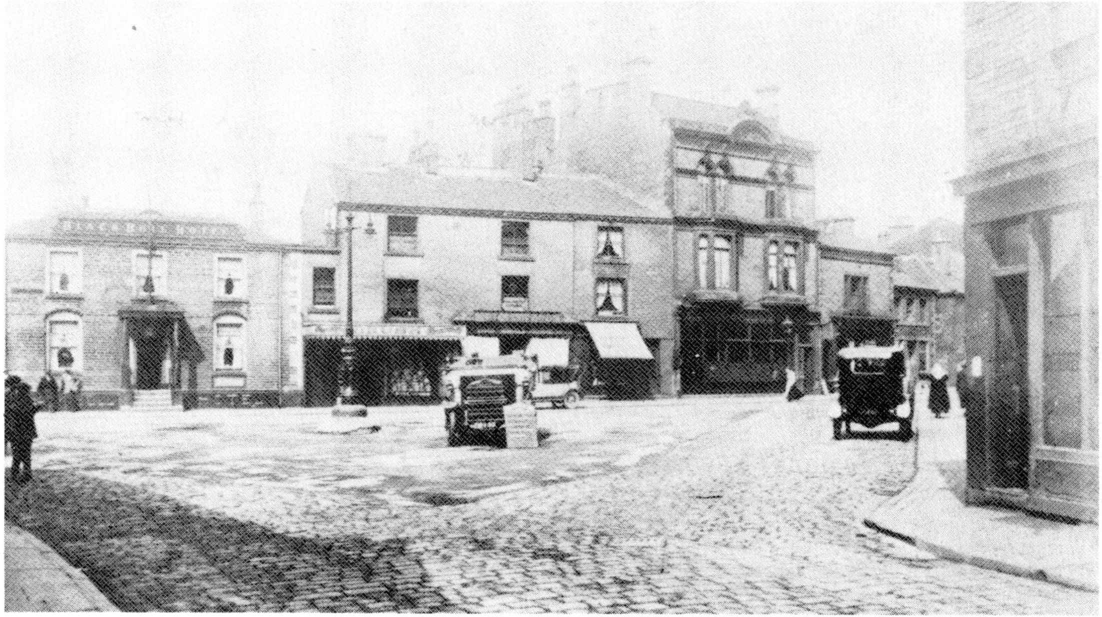

27. *Thornton Square.* From the market we move back to Bethel Street, but now looking into Briggate and the date is approximately 1925. As we can see, Holroyd Buildings had been demolished and Thornton Square had started to take shape. At the far side of the square we see Briggate as it was in those days and alas only the Black Bull to the left of the row of buildings is still standing. In the centre of the square stands a fifteen feet high ornamental lamp standard, with three arms and by the side of it is what looks like one of 'Tubba' Nelsons coaches; a sign-board of hiring charges along side. The automobile to the right is parked outside of the new Town Hall (municipal buildings) and here again we see Mr. Fox's shop on the extreme right. Nowadays this is where you will find the Midland Bank.

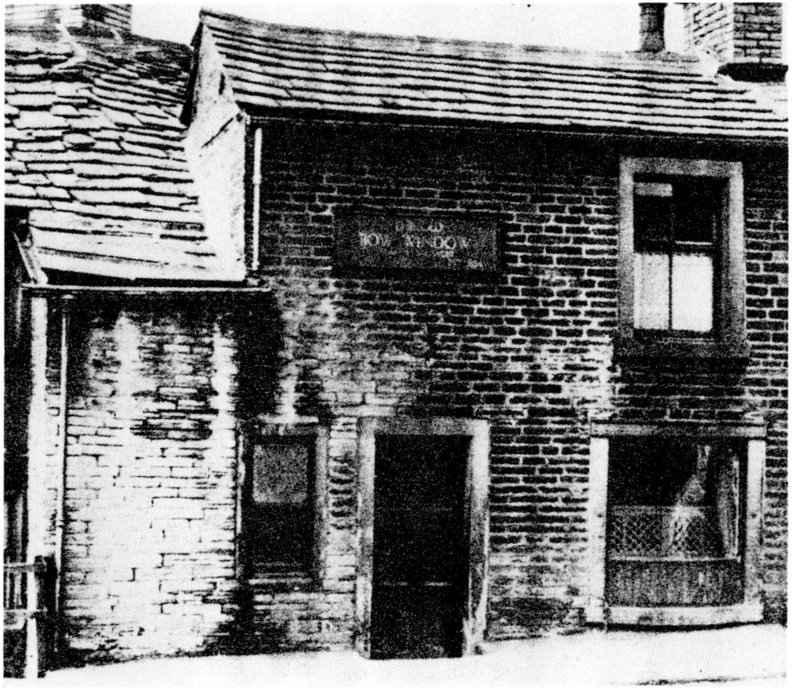

28. *The Old Bow Window.* Turning to the right and passing over Anchor Bridge, we come to an area of Briggate that used to be known as Queen Anne Square. It was here nearly opposite the Black Swan Inn, that the Stake Brothers set up a shop in 1864, probably the most popular place for a rendezvous. The Old Bow Window Restaurant sold brown or green peas, pies, sausages and the most succulent muffins at a very reasonable price. Down the steps, into a stone-flagged room with scrubbed wooden tables, was where you ate. To take-out, you could buy 'Half a muff dipped' for a halfpenny or sit in and have a dinner or supper to satisfy any appetite, for just a few 'coppers'. Rich and poor, young and old frequented this quaint little shop and it was a sad passing when it closed in the late 1950's, to be tarred over as a car park. An old postcard advertisement showed three thin men entering the shop and three fat men leaving – no idle boast according to folk who ate there.

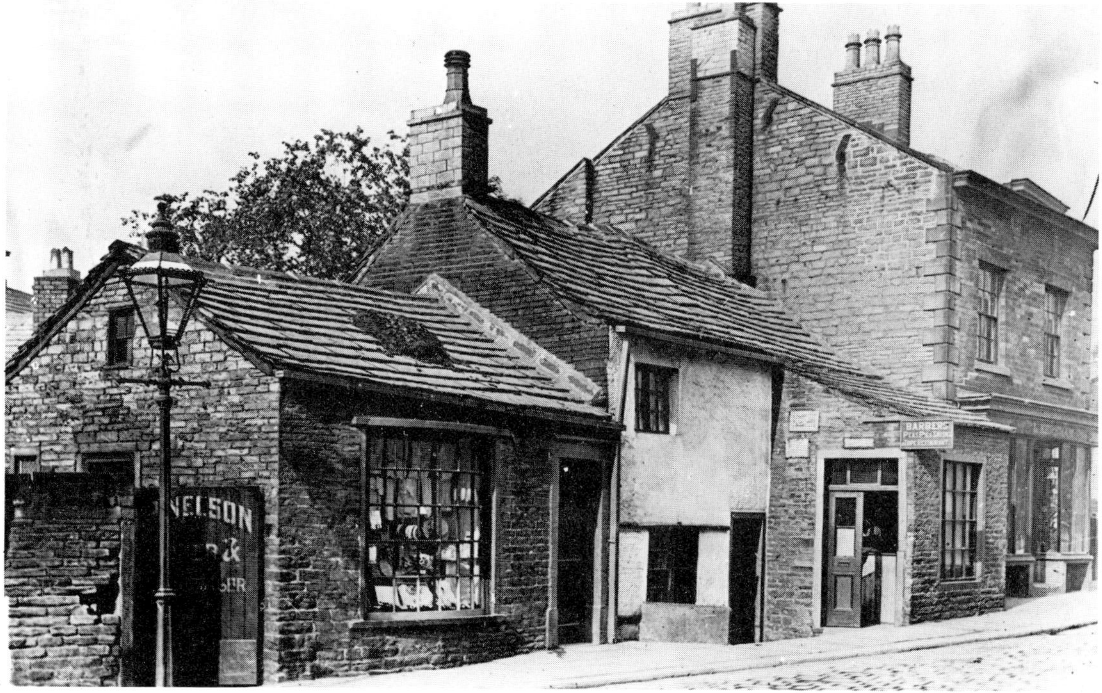

29. *Lower Briggate.* J.P. or 'Tubba' Nelson as he was known; his name appears on the wooden gate, by the lamp post in this picture, he was a cooper and cask dealer. He also had another string to his bow, that of running a coach business. He would ply for hire in Thornton Square advertising half-a-day trips for half-a-crown or a full day trip for five 'bob'; twenty-five newpence. A little further along was Barbers peas, pies, sausage and tripe restaurant where you could buy a beautiful tripe with lashings of vinager. Just a few years after this photograph was taken, this shop became Frances fish-shop. This whole site was where the Grand Clothing Hall, which later became the Astoria Ballroom, was built. In 1959 the area was levelled as part of the car park development previously mentioned.

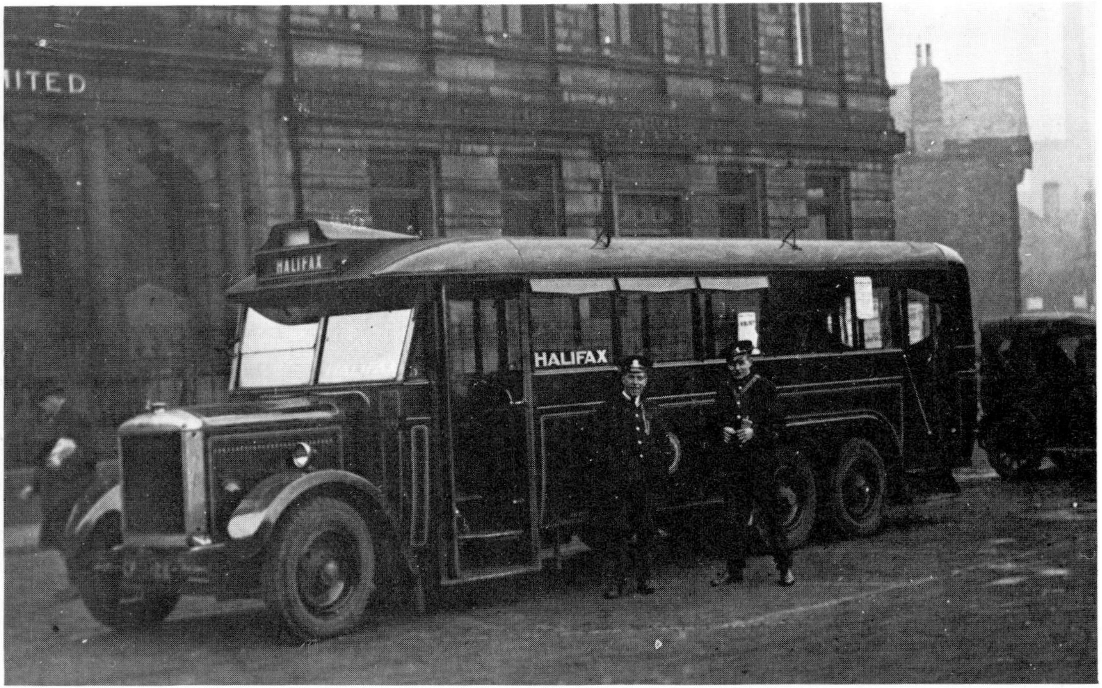

30. *Motor-bus.* When Thornton Square was laid out in front of the new Town Hall, all the motor-buses of the town were asked to use it as a place to pick up any passengers, but the square being rather small it soon became congested. Owler Ings Road was tried, but finally the council authorised the use of the Borough Market as a temporary bus station. 'The Karrier', the first six-wheeler bus to be used in Brighouse, ran from Thornton Square to Karrier Street in Halifax. The driver and conductor wore a smart, dark red livery, and could only issue return tickets as they were not allowed to pick up passengers outside the borough along the way. The Karrier was soon taken out of service as it could only manage to do six miles to the gallon. The Town Hall behind was opened in March 1887 as the municipal buildings. Brighouse already had a Town Hall, in Bradford Road, but extra accommodation was needed, and all the administration moved here later, making the old Town Hall the Civic Hall. A clock was added around 1920, a gift from Robert Thornton.

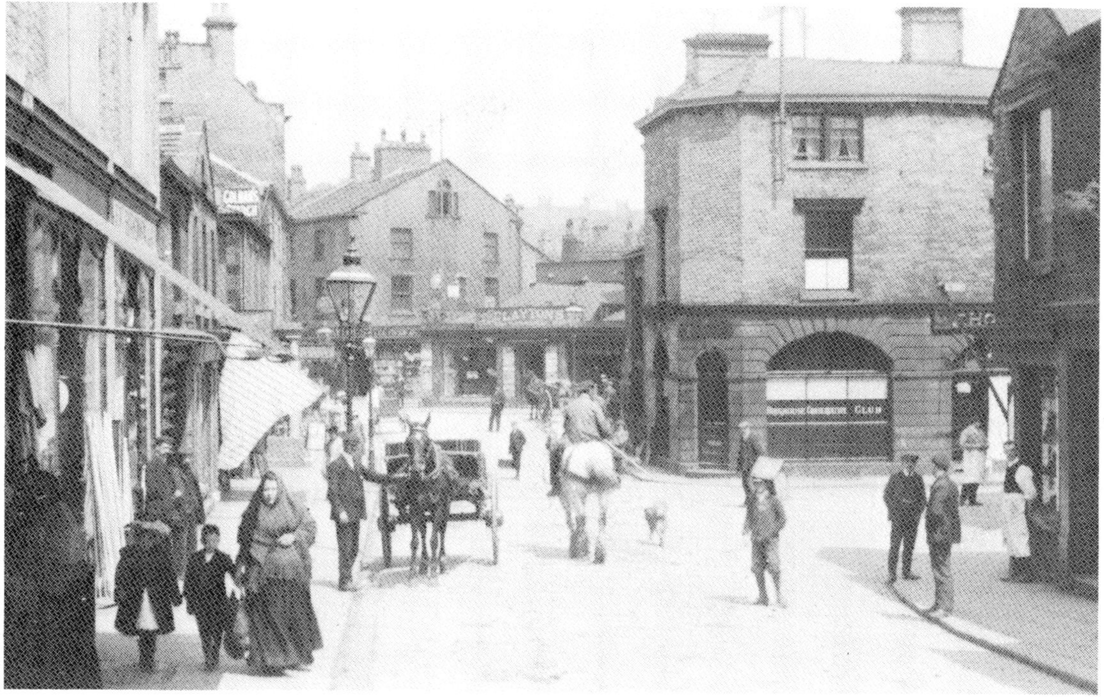

31. *Briggate.* This is another view of Briggate, looking towards Commercial Street around the turn of the century. It is almost unrecognisable by todays scene, as this part of the town has undergone the most change. On the left is John Francis Browns new shop, that was opened in 1904 and closed just a few years ago, re-opening as Oddjobs. In the centre is Claytons Central Mart, next door to the National Savings Centre; part of the municipal buildings, just out of sight, behind Holroyd Buildings. Claytons later moved their shop to Commercial Street when this site was cleared for the bus station. It is now the site of the Job Centre. The local Conservative Club was housed on this side of triangle, Holroyd Buildings, which was pulled down in 1914.

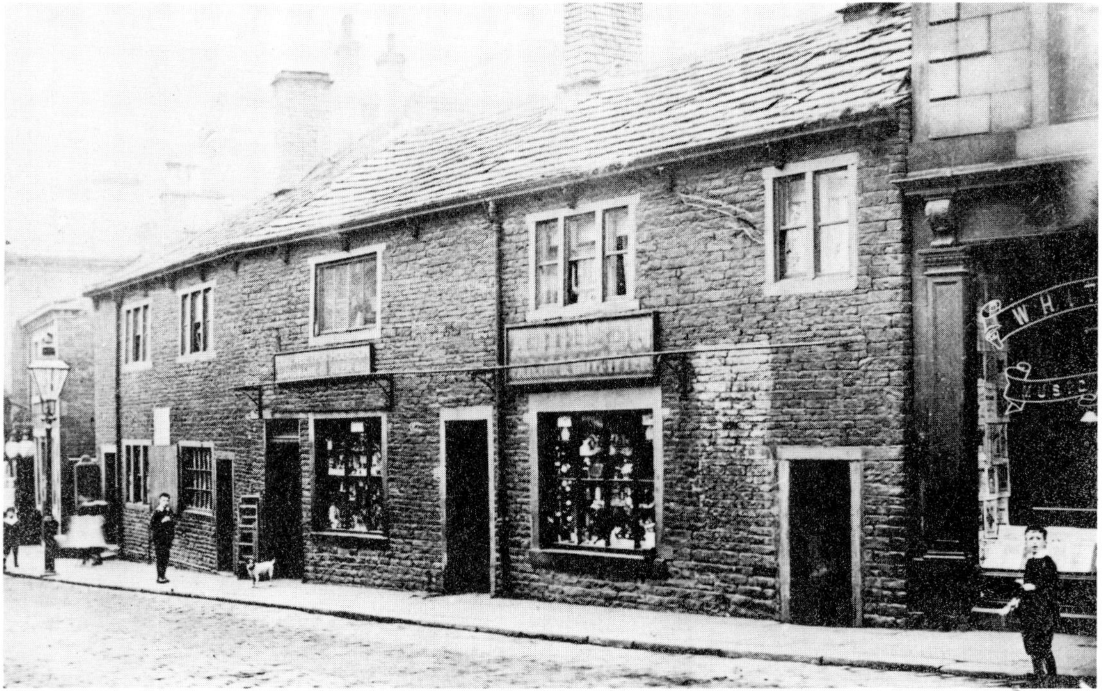

32. *Old Shops.* Moving along Briggate towards Commercial Street, on the left hand side around 1910 the shops used to look like this. The shop with the little dog outside of its door was owned by a hardware dealer by the name of Elizabeth J. Hodgson. Next door Martin Manley had his tailors and outfitters emporium, which in later years became an opticians shop. You could purchase spectacle frames from Woolworths and take them along to this shop to have your own specific lenses fitted. On the right, partly out of our picture, was Whitfields Music Shop, that later became a fancy goods store. All of this area was cleared to make way for the big Hillards Supermarket when they moved from Commercial Street.

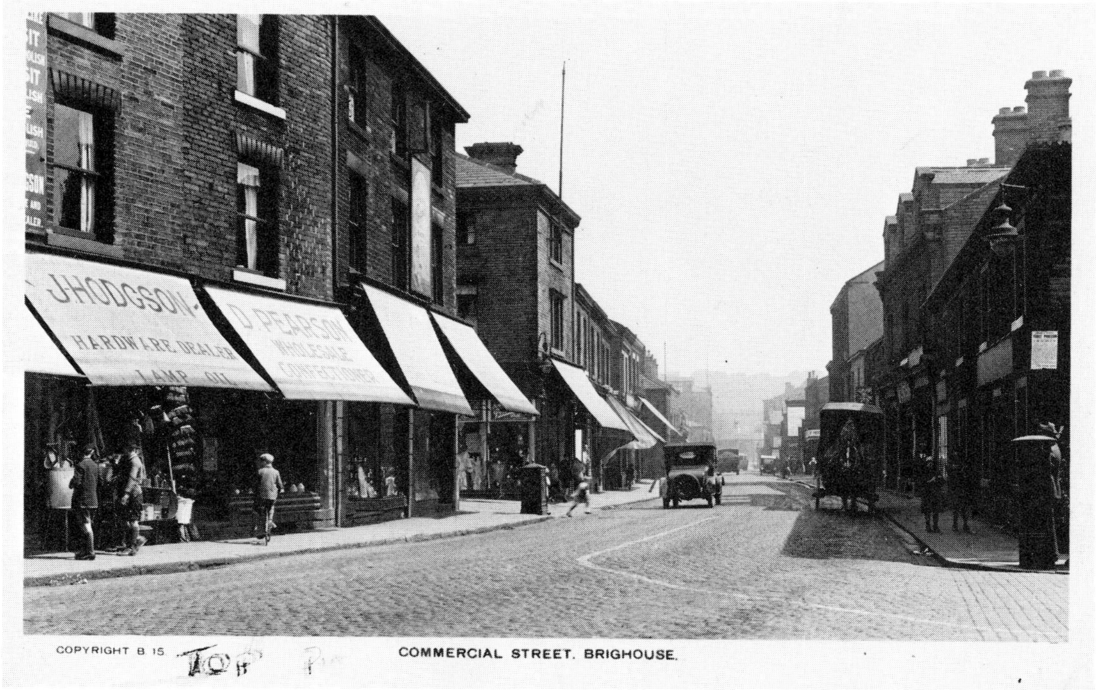

33. *Commercial Street.* Towards the end of Briggate, we turn to the right into Commercial Street that will lead us back to the George Corner. To the left in this picture postcard we find that the hardware dealer Elizabeth J. Hodgson had moved premises from Briggate. Other shops that could be seen further along Commercial Street in 1905 were The Maypole, the first of the large multiple stores and James Joys, where you could buy a very reliable timepiece. At the far end of the street can be seen Taylors chemist shop and about halfway along the right hand side is a well-known advertisement sign for Singer Sewing Machines. In this view also only one lamp post can be seen, at the bottom of Church Lane. Another lamp is hanging at the corner on the right; this one would be owned by the Wellington Hotel.

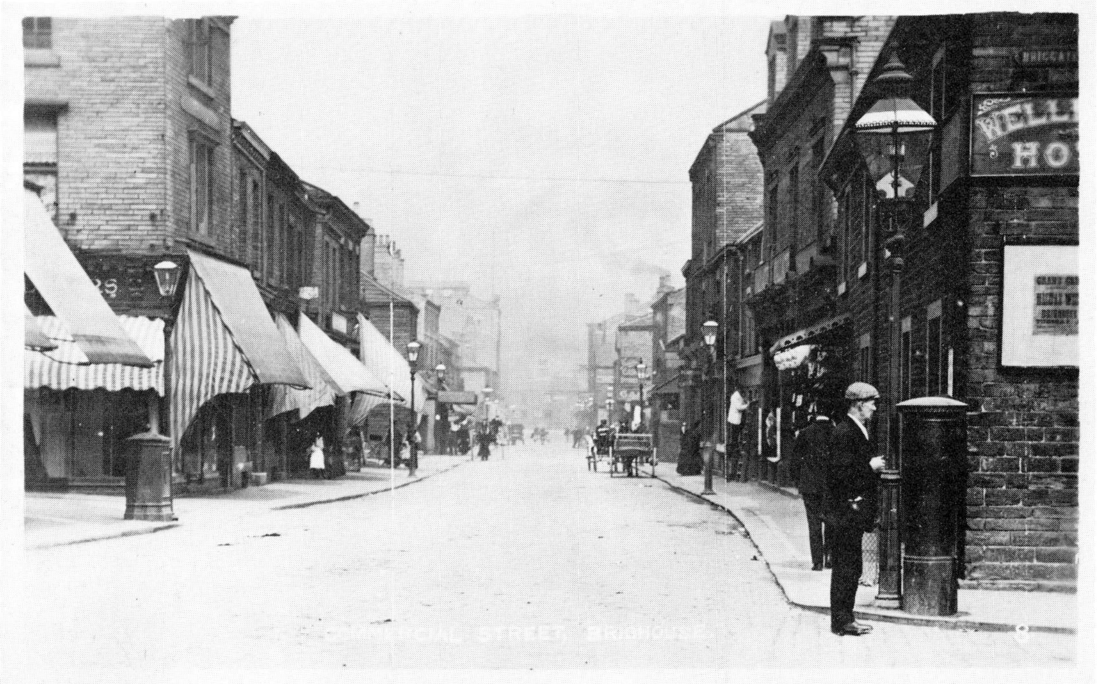

34. *Wellington Hotel.* Turning slightly into Commercial Street and travelling in time about fifteen years, we can now see the gas lamps all the way along the street. These were installed in 1913 by the borough council and worked on a clock-timing system. We can see that the Wellington Hotel which also had its own brewery at the rear of these premises, by the way, had dismantled its own lamp as it was no longer needed. On the left is old Hamers shop and two shops along was George Mitchells boot and shoe shop. Claytons dress shop sign can be just about seen jutting out over the pavement, about halfway along the left hand side. On the right side, after the Wellington Hotel is the Cash Fruit Stores, the Ring O'Bells, that used to be called the Staff of Life, until the Parish Church received its first peel of bells; J.P.'s; Heywoods and then Lancaster fish and fruit shop.

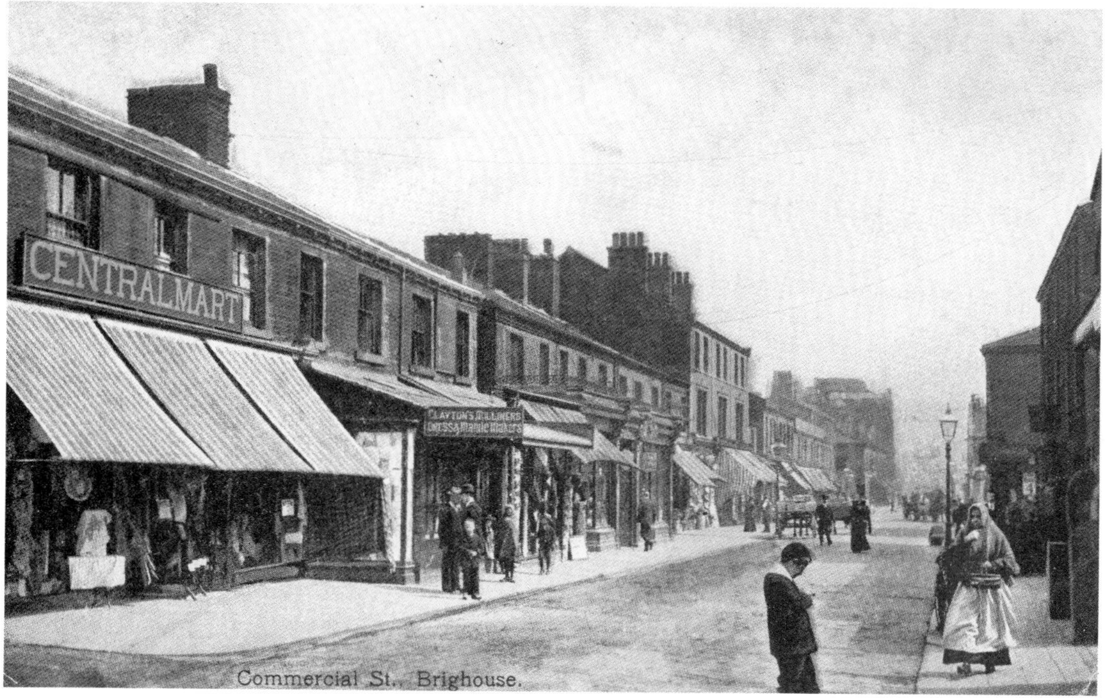

35. *Central Mart.* The date of this card is 1904 and we are now in Commercial Street across from the bottom of Hutchinson Lane. Here, in full view, is Claytons Central Mart and Milliner dress shop and mantle makers. You could purchase a jumper in crêpe-de-chine from nine shillings and eleven pence to fifteen shillings each. The area on the right contained Frank Newtons butchers shop next to Nettletons Yard. Then there was a tripe shop owned by Marshells, which for some reason had bars on the windows; who would want to pinch tripe? Sharpes the saddlers came next; Thomas Ives grocery and then the labyrinth of passageways known as 'Zingo Nick'. Then came Websters pawnshop and then Sam Marshells grocers shop before we reach Park Street. This whole section was cleared in 1932 to make room for Market Street and more modern shops including the first Woolworths in Brighouse.

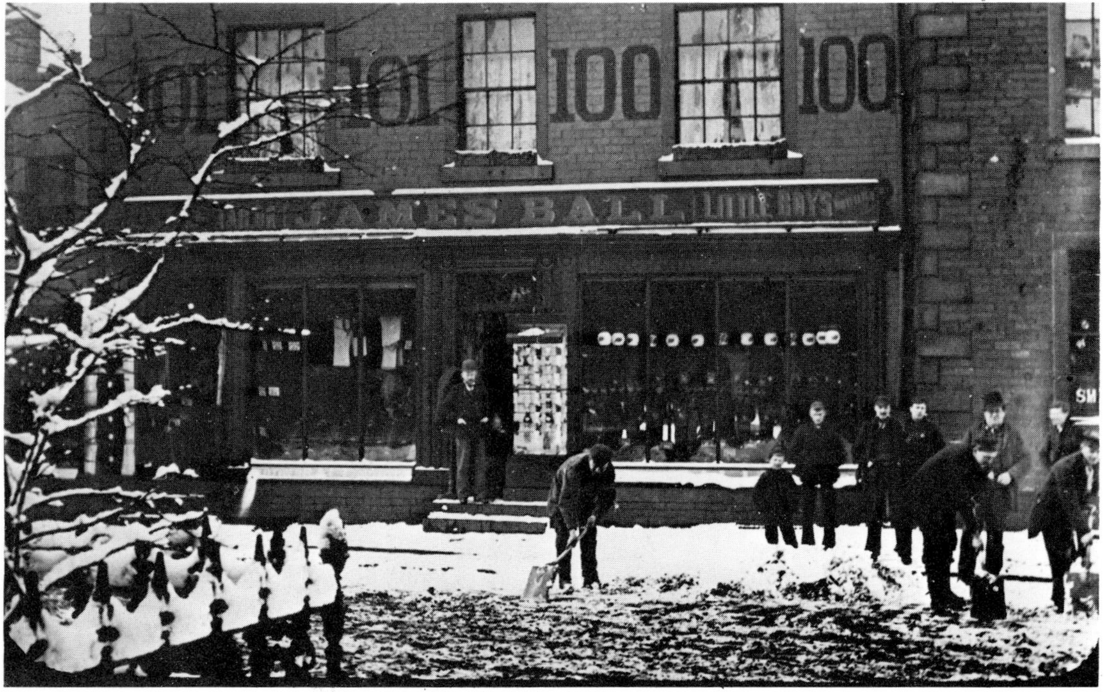

36. *James Ball.* Moving right along Commercial Street, we now go even further back in time to 1886 and find Mr. James Ball's emporium. He liked his shop to be known not only as a gents tailors but also as a little boys tailors too. His shop was right next door to the George Hotel and you can see the Georges smoke-room at the edge of the picture. It was around this area that the Irish riots of 1882 erupted. News of the assassination of one of the districts representatives in parliament, Lord Frederick Cavendish, killed by Irish extremists, reached the Brighouse people. Crowds rampaged through the streets with much rough handling, damages and looting done to the Irish contingent and their property. Policemen were drafted in from neighbouring districts, some were attacked and beaten, but eventually after the riot act had been read to a crowd that had gathered outside the Town Hall, peace was restored to the town.

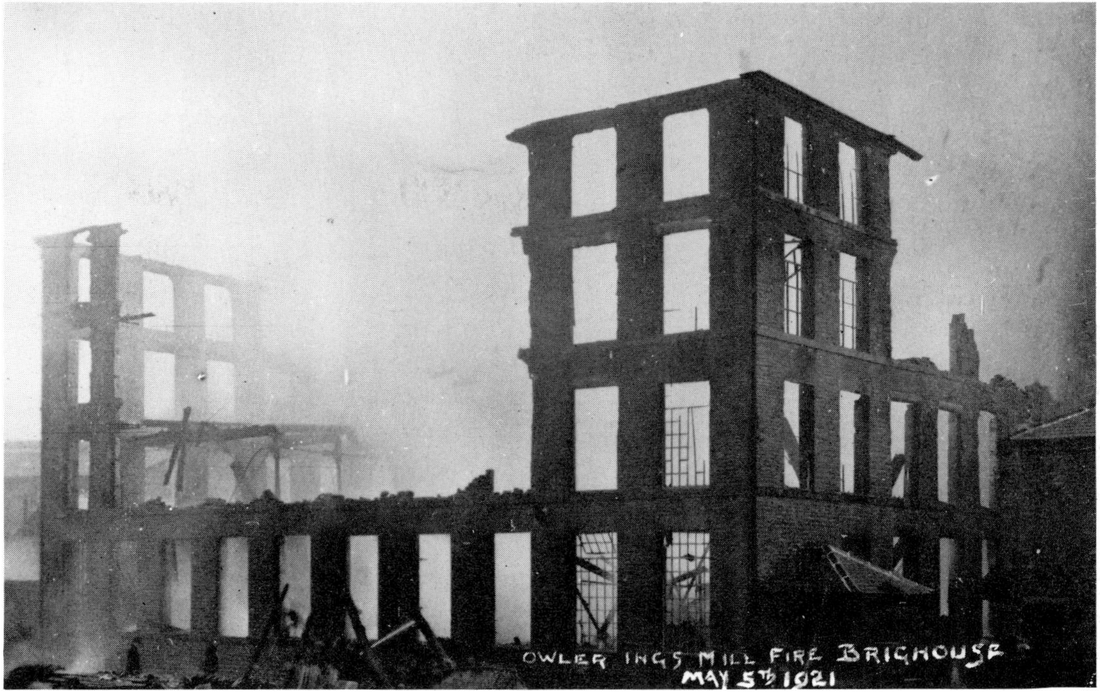

37. *Owler Ings Mill.* Owler Ings Mill, behind Briggate to the east, was built in two sections by T.T. Ormerod, his architect being George Hepworth. The section next to the canal was finished in 1862 and the second, larger part, on Owler Ings Road, in 1865. Later various firms used parts of the building for cotton doubling and worsted spinning and two fires were successfully put out by some good work by the Brighouse Fire Brigade. In 1920 the mill was renovated and extended to include a sprinkler tower, unfortunately when the above fire took place the water supply had not been connected. From start to finish, the whole mill was gutted in just over an hour; a breeze helping to fan the flames. Clothing and wages of some of the workers had to be left behind as they scrambled for their lives. Six fire crews attended the fire, but were helpless against the conflagration. Although 130 were added to the unemployment list, not one person was injured in the whole incident.

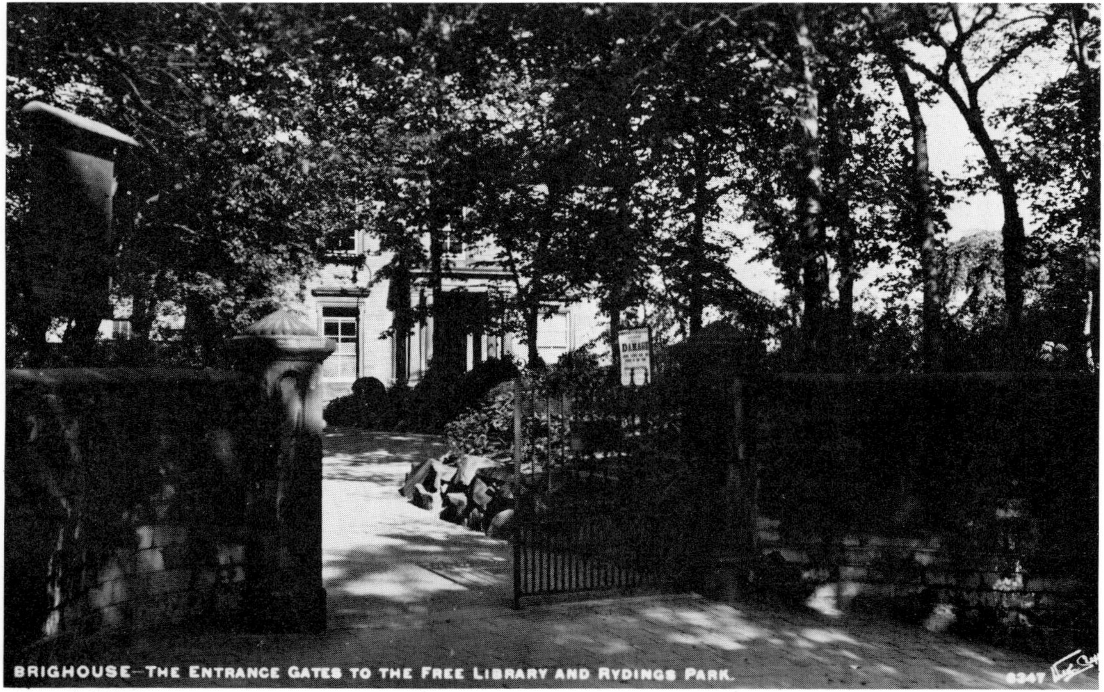

38. *Library Entrance.* From the west end of Commercial Street, Halifax Road extends Northward towards Hipperholme. The entrance to the Rydings is halfway up 'John King Lane' as the first stretch of Halifax Road is known by most locals. John King Lane acquired its name from a gentleman of that name who was greatly involved with the running of Brighouse before the local board was formed. John King died in 1854 and his house which was situated near the bottom of the lane, was pulled down shortly after. This postcard shows the entrance to Rydings Park as it was when the Free Library was first opened. Where have all the lovely trees disappeared to to-day?

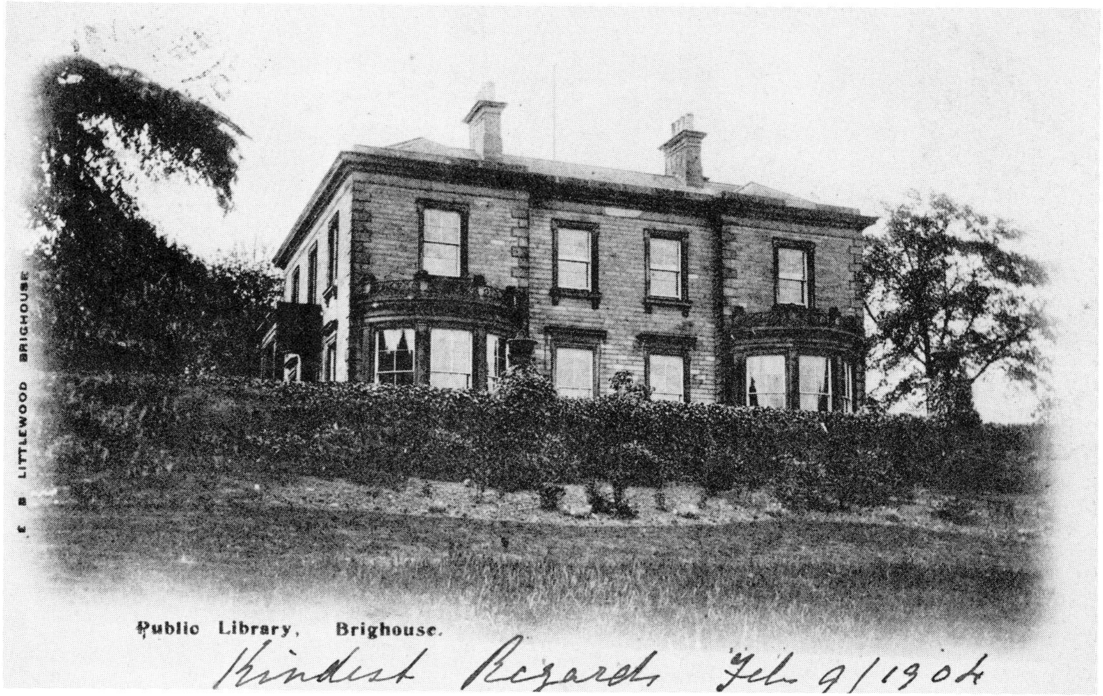

39. *Public Library*. Brighouse was fortunate to have had a library as early as 1784, when the Brighouse Subscription Library was established, and lasted throughout the greater part of the nineteenth century. There was also a reading room full of books that had been set up by the Mechanics Institute on Bethel Street. In 1895 the Library Association wrote to the Brighouse Town Council suggesting that they start a free lending library. The Rydings was purchased by public subscription, as part of the Queen Victoria Diamond Jubilee celebrations, to house the books, among them a large collection of Yorkshire books which were donated by a local historian of the time, J. Horsfall Turner. The library was opened by the Marquis of Ripon in June 1898.

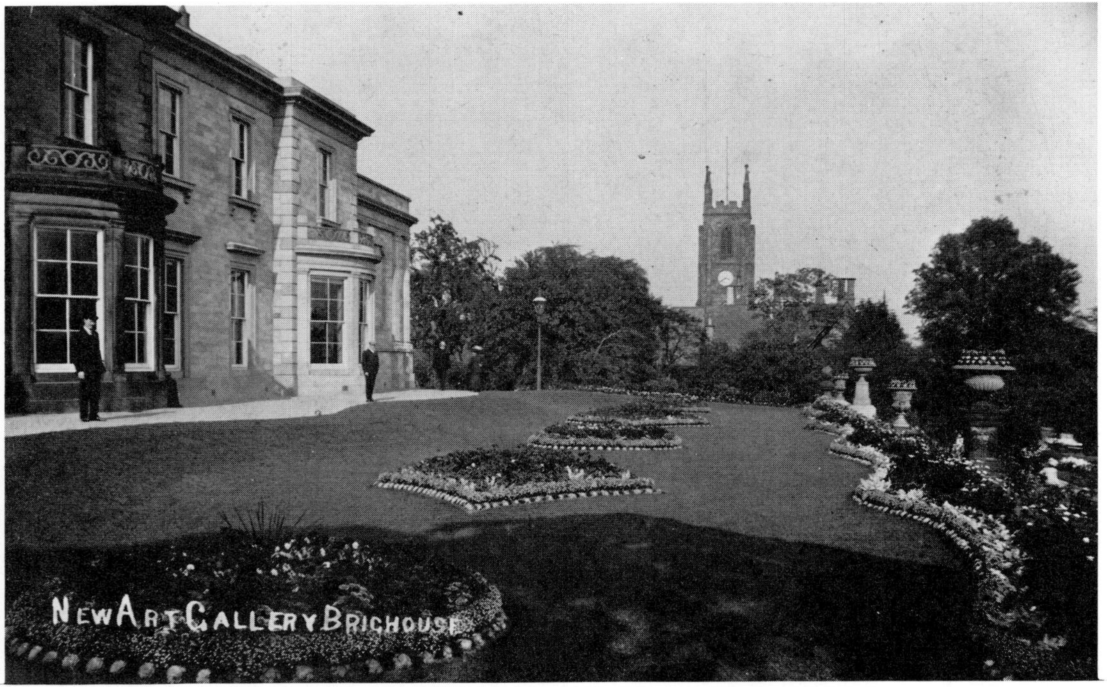

40. *New Art Gallery*. The Rydings is believed to have been built about 1841 by John Brooke, a local corn miller. In 1903 Miles Sharp, a native artist of Brighouse, held an exhibition of his work at the library. These exhibitions became a regular thing with local and national artists participating, so William Smith, the mayor at that time, had an extention built onto the Rydings, to house the art gallery and a reading room. It was decided that Princess Louise, Duchess of Argyle and Queen Victoria's daughter, should open the gallery, but four councillors voted against spending £120 to entertain her. The gallery was opened in 1907. In the background can be seen the parish church of St. Martin's, built as a result of an Act of Parliament dated 1818 known as the 'Million Pound Act'. The act made money available to build new churches in industrial areas. A full peal of bells was added in 1847 and to celebrate, a public house across from the bottom of Church Lane called 'The Staff of Life' changed its name to 'The Ring of Bells'.

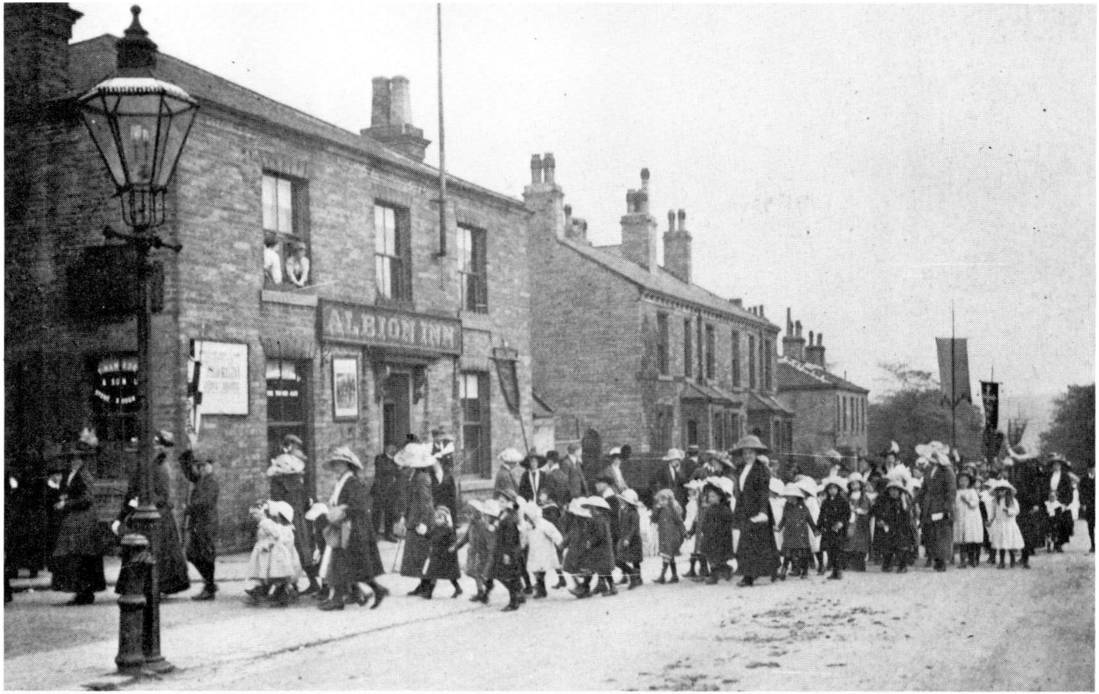

41. *Albion Inn.* At the top of John King Lane or the first rise of Halifax Road, stands the Albion Inn, once owned by Altie Farrar, a great rugby and cricket player in his day. The Albion was one of the first public houses in Brighouse to install a full size billiards table. The exterior of the pub looks quite different today as it has a large entrance porch. The area is known as Lane Head and Lane Head recreation ground was at the back of the albion, at first, but was later moved about a hundred yards further up Halifax Road. The photograph, circa 1905, is of a Whit walk, when all the church schools took part, with the children dressed in their best 'bib and tucker'. The boys wore short trousers, a rounded jacket with a belt-round waist, a linen collar and a bow tie. The hair was worn long and brushed and oiled. The girls also had an awkward style, with long dresses well below the knees and woollen stockings.

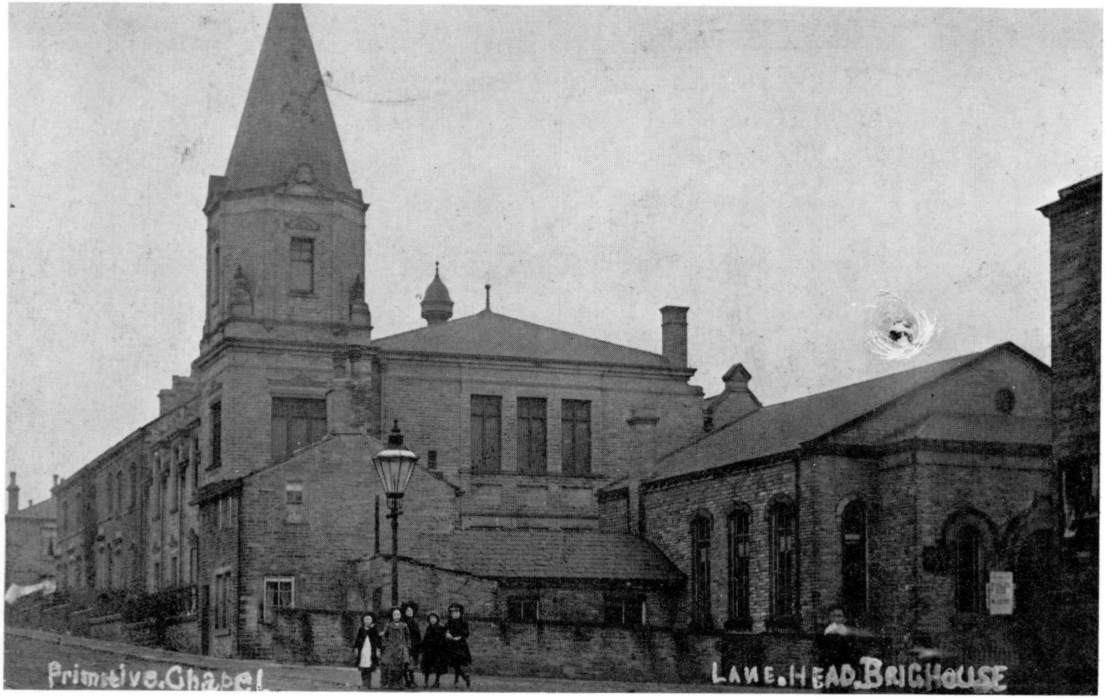

42. *Lane Head Chapel.* When the toll charges on the old turnpike roads were abolished around 1864, the Brighouse Primitive Methodists purchased the no longer needed bar-house at Lane Head, on the opposite side of Waterloo Road to the Albion Inn. They incorporated it as part of the chapel that they built there, at a cost of £811. It was Nathan Robinson who brought Primitive Methodism to Brighouse and at its inception held meetings at his own house in Thornhill Briggs. In June a larger building was built as the new chapel, leaving the old chapel for usage as the Sunday School. Due to a combination of the amalgamation of the Methodist Church under one body and the drop in attendance, this chapel was closed in the 1970s and was demolished in 1986, leaving a small house which still contains the old bar-house.

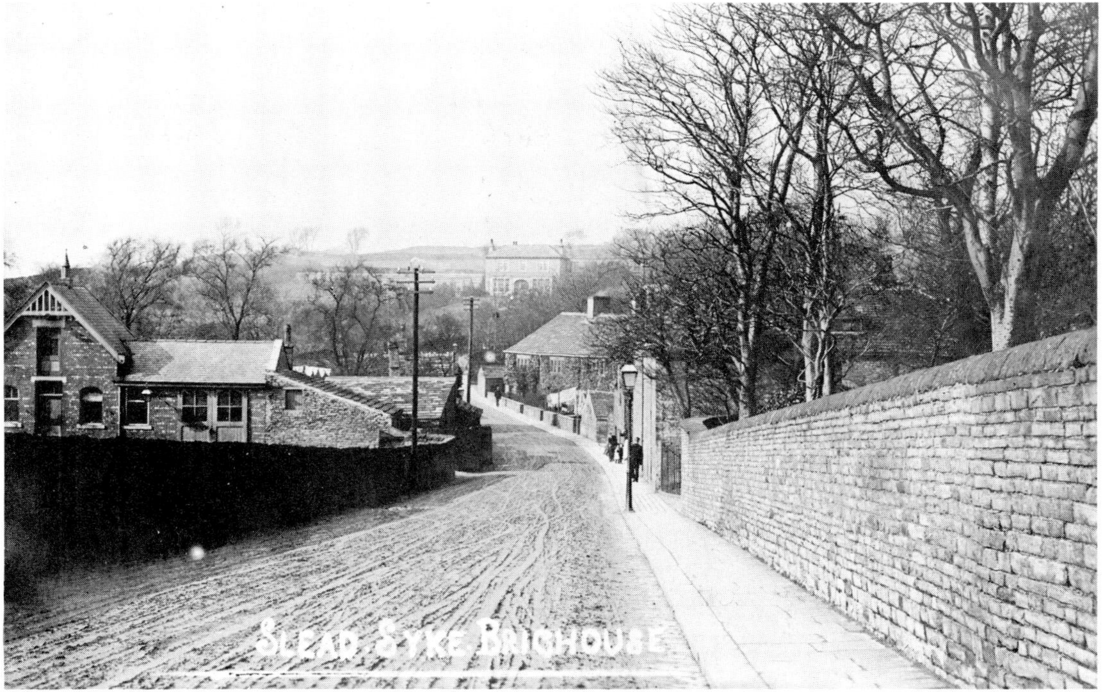

43. *Slead Syke.* As we proceed along Halifax Road, we come to the area known as Slead Syke. The word slead is said to derive from a Saxon word meaning 'wooded dell'; not a bad description looking at the postcard above. The building on the left is Dysons Farm and there is a mention of a Mr. James Dyson owning a wood in this area in 1769. All the land on the left-hand side of the road, including where Dysons Farm was, is now an abundance of housing except the section on the far rise, which is where Kershaw Garden Centre now is. In the trees on right opposite Kershaws, is Slead Hall, the present building dating back to 1636, but earlier ownerships of a house on this site are noted in 1571 selling for £60. The oak panelling in the house is believed to have been brought from New Hall in Elland. Granny Hall Lane has not as wide an entrance as it has nowadays, opening just passed the lamp-post.

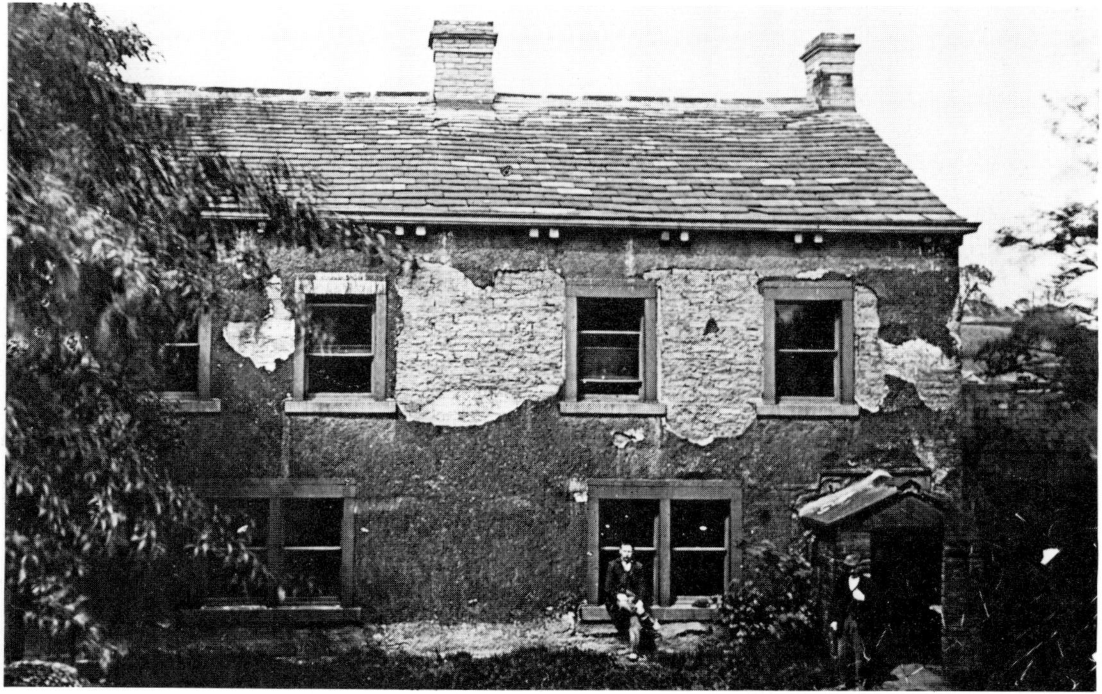

44. *Granny Hall.* Here we have a dilapidated old house, photographed just before it was pulled down in 1907. About halfway along Granny Hall Lane, where Blackburn Road leads off to the bottom end of Lane Head recreation ground, is where Granny Hall used to be situated, with grounds that covered the new metalled road that we have today. The last owner of the house was one J. Horsfall Turner F.R.H.S., a local historian who wrote a book called 'The History of Brighouse, Rastrick and Hipperholme' which was first printed in 1893. A recent re-issue of the book came out in 1986 and has helped me to compile my notes for this book. Most of Granny Hall Lane is now built up, but the place where the hall was, has now been made into a garden of rest, with a lawn and roses all set out.

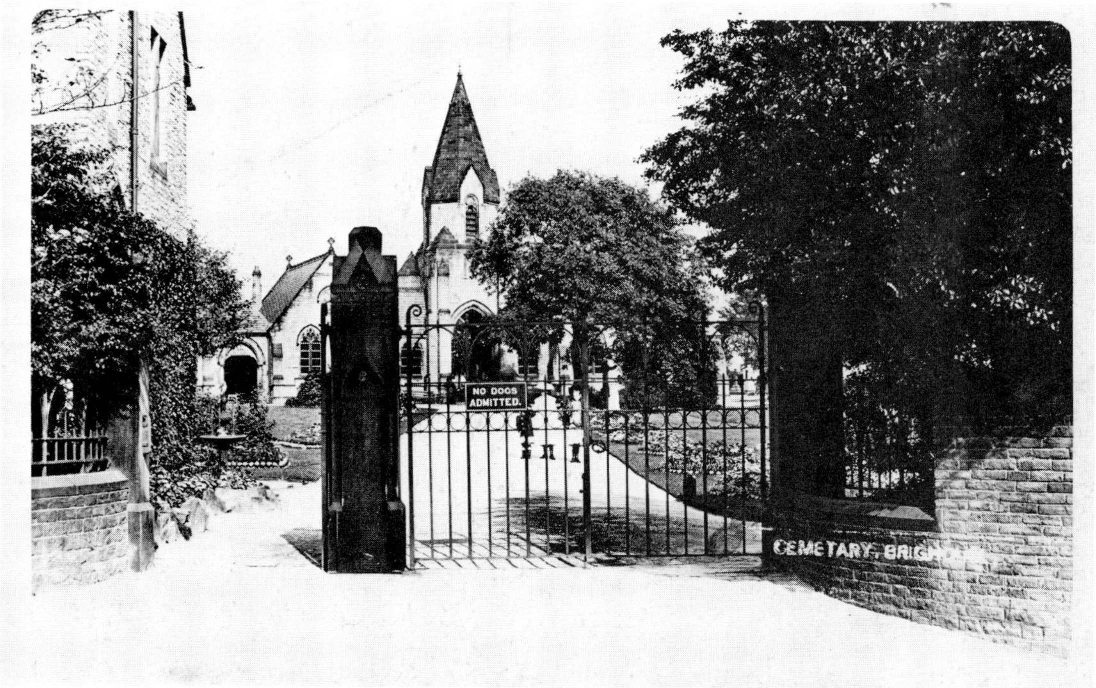

45. *Brighouse Cemetery*. Continuing along Granny Hall Lane we come to the crossroads with Lightcliffe Road and turning left up this road we come to the Brighouse cemetery gates, on our right. By the end of 1869 the Parish Church burial ground was becoming so full, that claims were being made, that people were being buried in the wrong graves. Complaints of overcrowding had been put before the local board for a number of years but they had been very slow at setting up a burial board. Eventually the board was organised and after a lot of wrangling, the cemetery was ready for use and was consecrated by the Bishop of Ripon in 1874. A prize had been offered for the best designer of the cemetery chapel, this being won by William Gray of Bradford. The flower gardens and shrubbery were laid out and planted by Lister Kershaw.

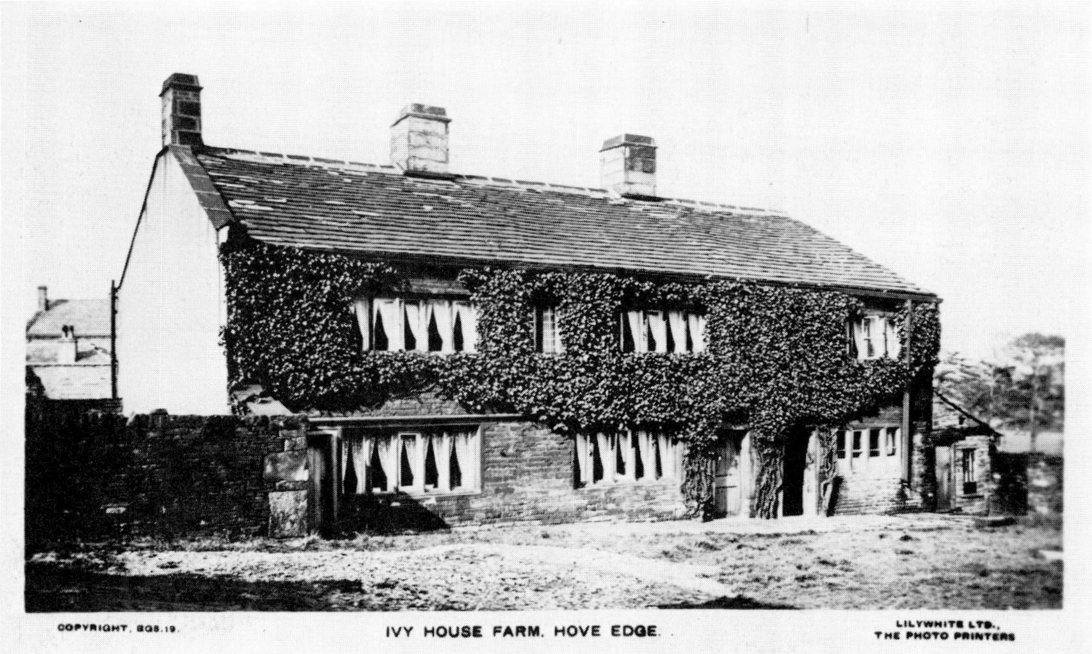

46. *Ivy House Farm.* Lightcliffe Road leads us back to Halifax Road, but before we come to this junction we have entered Hove Edge. John Wesley visited the Hipperholme-cum-Brighouse district three times in his ministry, staying at Smith House in Lightcliffe, and would probably have preached in this farm house at some time. Strife split the Methodist society, when there was a dispute between the followers of Wesley and the Reverend Alex Kelhams supporters. The local leader of the Wesleyans was John Sharp who lived at Ivy House Farm and for a time the Wesleyans worshipped in his front parlour, the New Connection having taken over Park Chapel. There is a reference on the plan of the Halifax Methodist Circuit dated 1802, to a preaching house at Hove Edge; no doubt Ivy House Farm. After a legal battle in 1810 the Wesleyans were able to reclaim Park Chapel and moved to the centre of Brighouse. The above postcard shows the farm and though it is not much changed today, do you know where it is? With houses all around, St. Chads school on its right-hand side and Well Green Lane boundary wall to its front quite a number of people living in Hove Edge do not know.

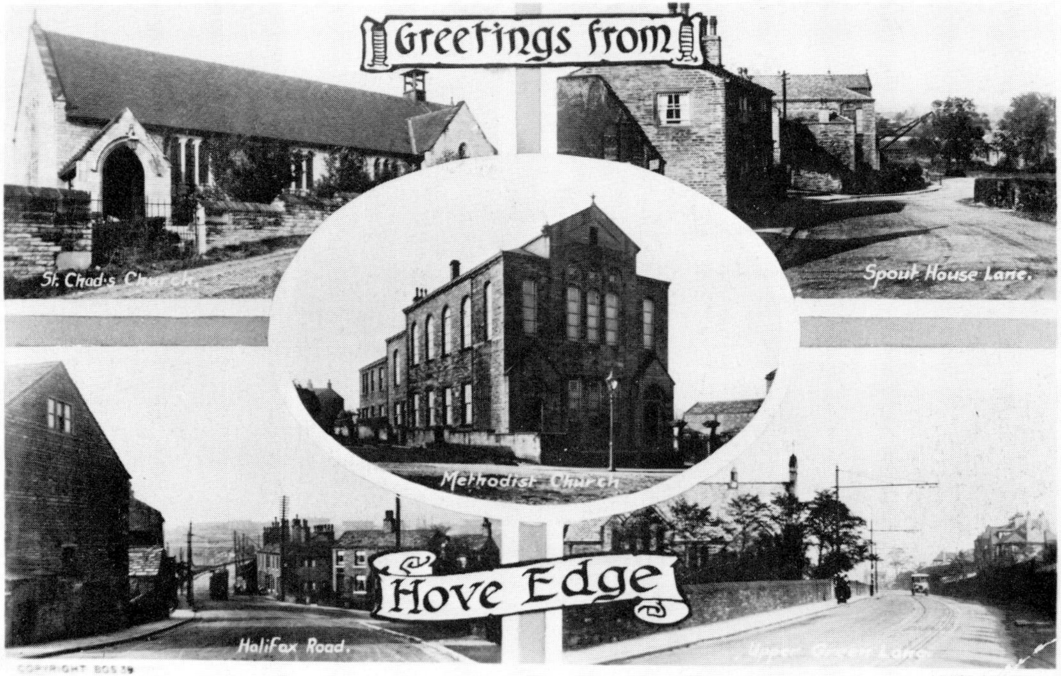

47. *Methodist Church (centre)*. Just around the corner from Ivy House Farm, on Spout House Lane, the Zion Methodist Free Church was built in 1882. In 1880 a new body of trustees was formed, consisting of seven delvers, a silk spinner, a silk dresser, a stone mason, a brass finisher, a plumber and an architect. These men were inspired to purchase 870 square yards of land at this spot from Mr. R. Wood, Lightcliffe for £152. The Ancient Order of Foresters, who at that time met at the Black Bull in Brighouse, loaned the trustees £500 to help build the church, which had a total cost of £2,500 for the building and furnishings. A pipe-organ was later purchased from a cotton spinner of West Vale, who had had the thing erected in his house, but no longer used it. Its cost of £300 was defrayed by the charge of one and sixpence to watch the installation. Due again to falling attendances, it was inevitable that some chapels would have to close their doors. The Zion Church, however, lasted one hundred years, but was finally pulled down in the 1970s and replaced by housing.

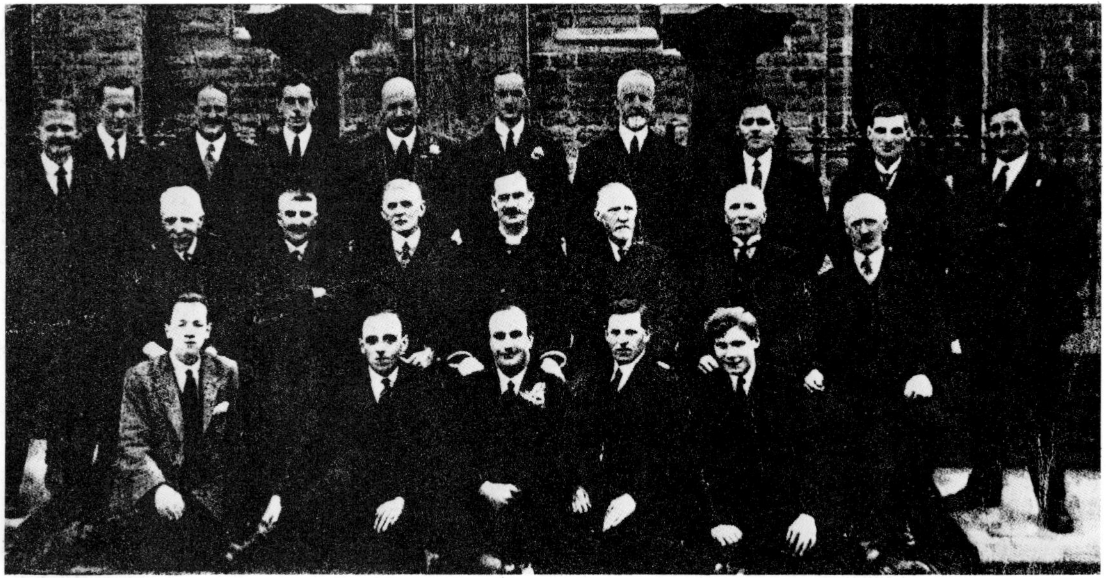

48. *Trustees*. The above picture is of a new body of trustees elected in 1923 to organise the Diamond Jubilee year of the Zion Church. The objective was to purchase a new organ, renovate the chapel by installing electricity and covering the new pew seats with material. This was accomplished over a three week-end project, with musical services, a lovefeast and an old scholars re-union to raise some extra money. The members of the Trustees in this photograph are left to right, back row: Harry Taylor, Medley Fisher, Wilfred Oates, Leonard Aspinall, Ernest Armitage, Herbert Armitage, Sam Bottomley, Leonard Oates, Amos Pinder and Benny Oates. Middle row: Alfred Hardy, Edward Aspinall, James Mosey, Reverend J. Ninnis, Robert F. Rogerson, George Walker and Joseph H. Hardy. Front row: George Marsden, Ernest Green, John Armitage, Herbert Beevers and Leonard Collins.

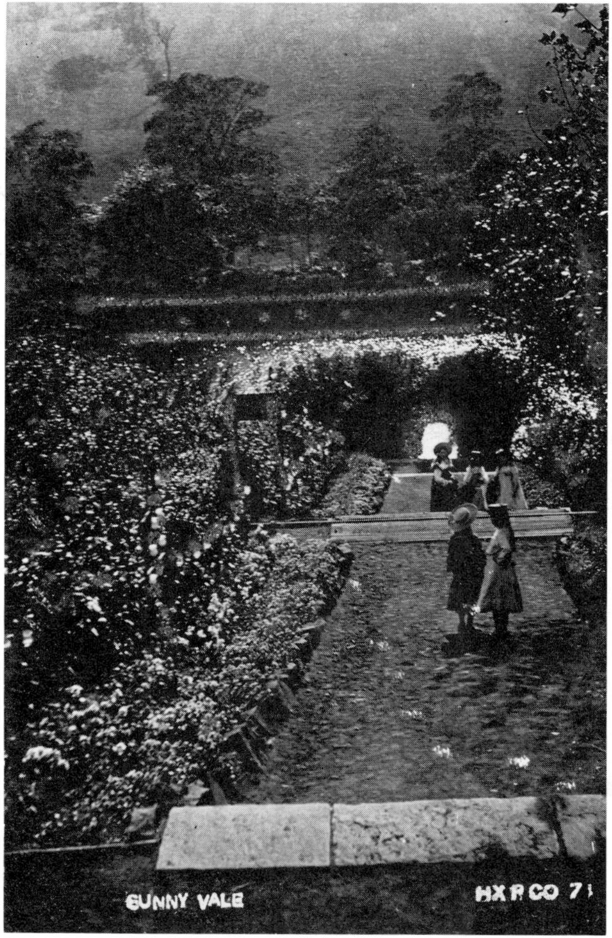

49. *Sunny Vale.* We have now moved over Halifax Road and down Half House Lane towards the Shibden valley and Shibden Hall, but first we come to the Sunny Vale pleasure gardens which was a popular place for an outing. Joseph Bunce was born in 1850 and first came to live at Wood Bottom Farm in 1880, where his intention was to start a market garden on the two acres of land. Known as 'Sunny Bunces', the popular resort in the Waterclough valley, close to Hipperholme Station, soon became the place to visit if you were in the area. Bunce constructed two lakes, a maize and even purchased from the Bradford Exhibition 'The Palace of Illusion', which he re-erected in Sunny Vale. On Easter Monday 1903 10,000 people turned up to hear music by King Cross Band and watch the late night firework display. In September each year Councillor Bunce organised a water carnival and pageant, when the whole of the illuminated grounds took on the fantasy of a fairy grotto.

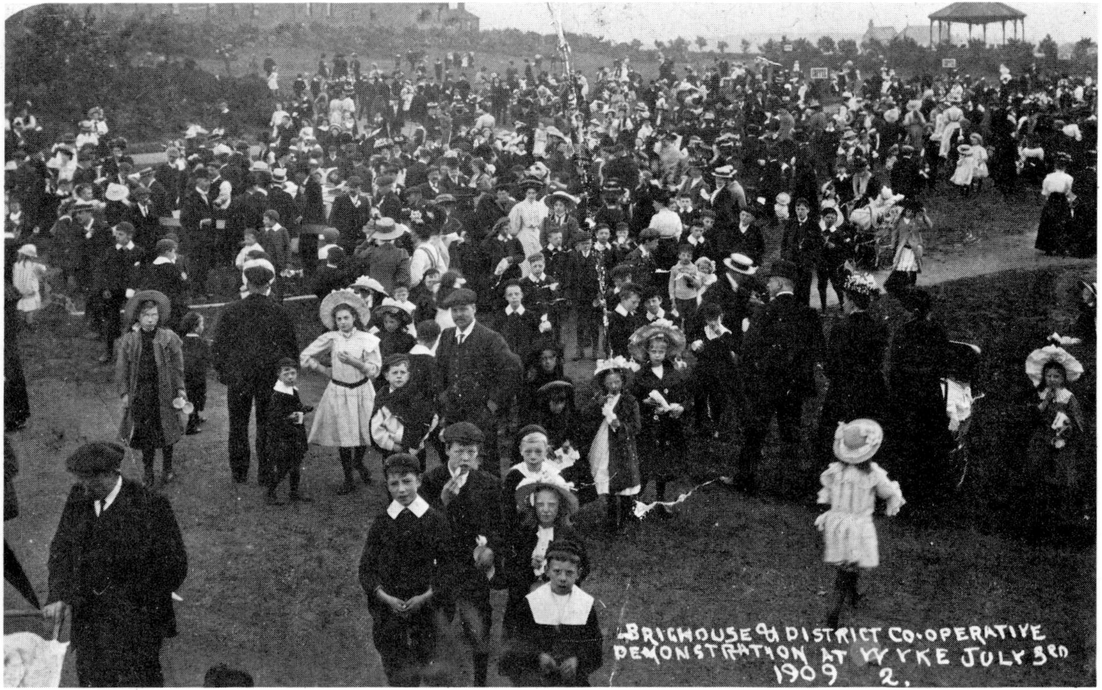

50. *Co-operative Demonstration.* The Brighouse and District Co-operative demonstration was an annual event that moved around the district that was served the 'Co-operators', as the members of the society were known. The Co-operative covered an area from Rastrict to Wyke and from Hipperholme to Clifton but on 3rd July 1909 the demonstration, which had nearly 3,000 children in attendance, was at Wyke. To transport all the children from Clifton, Hove Edge, Lightcliffe, Brookfoot, Oaks Green and Castle Hill, Rastrick, as well as from Brighouse, quite a number of coaches had to be drafted in. The children were served with coffee and buns in return for their one penny ticket, and then races of all kinds were organised for them to take part in, with prizes for the first three to past the post.

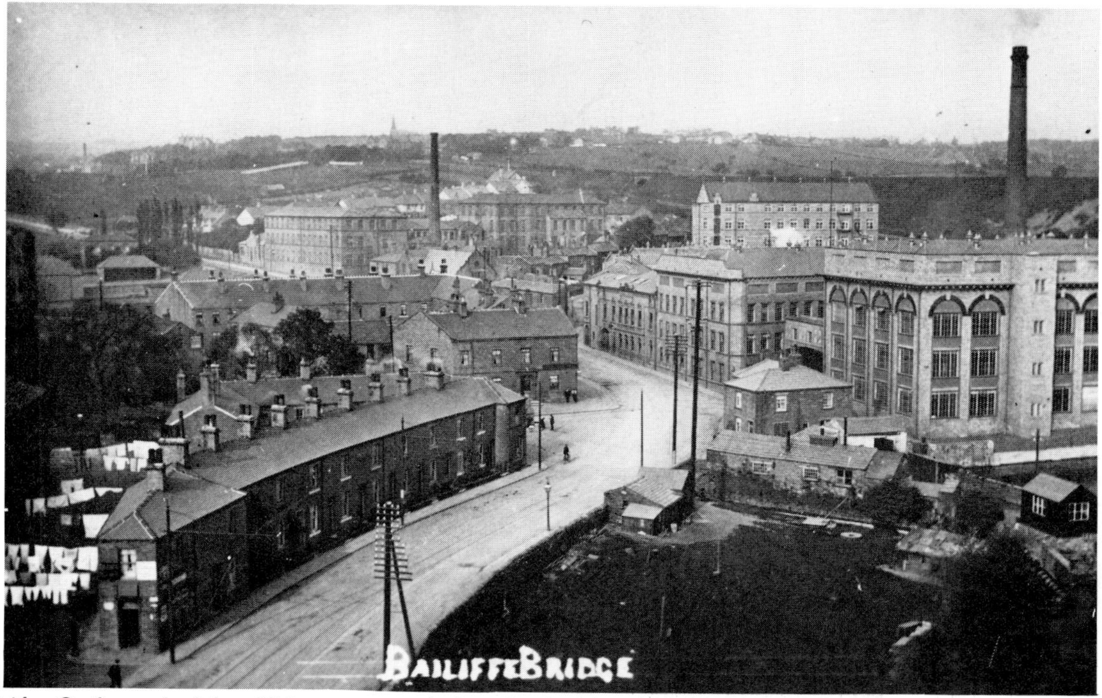

51. ***Bailiffe Bridge.*** **On the way back from Wyke, as we cross the boundary back into the Brighouse borough we** enter first the district of Bailiffe Bridge . In 1910 Lady Firth of Holme House offered to provide a drinking fountain for the centrepiece of the Bailiffe Bridge village. Consisting of two water troughs of solid granite and surrounded by an ornate fountain, with an iron-work lantern on top, this was completed and installed in 1911. Looking closely at the above postcard one can just see the edge of this fountain, at the far end of the bottom row of houses. It remained there, opposite Firths Carpet Mill for some fifty years. In 1913 the Bradford Corporation agreed to extend their Wyke tramway terminus to the corner beside the Punch Bowl Inn in the centre of the postcard. Up to this time, if you wanted to travel to Bradford from Brighouse, you had to catch a tram to Bailiffe Bridge and walk a mile to Wyke, before you could mount a tram to Bradford. Both of the chimneys and quite a number of the buildings in this picture, have disappeared.

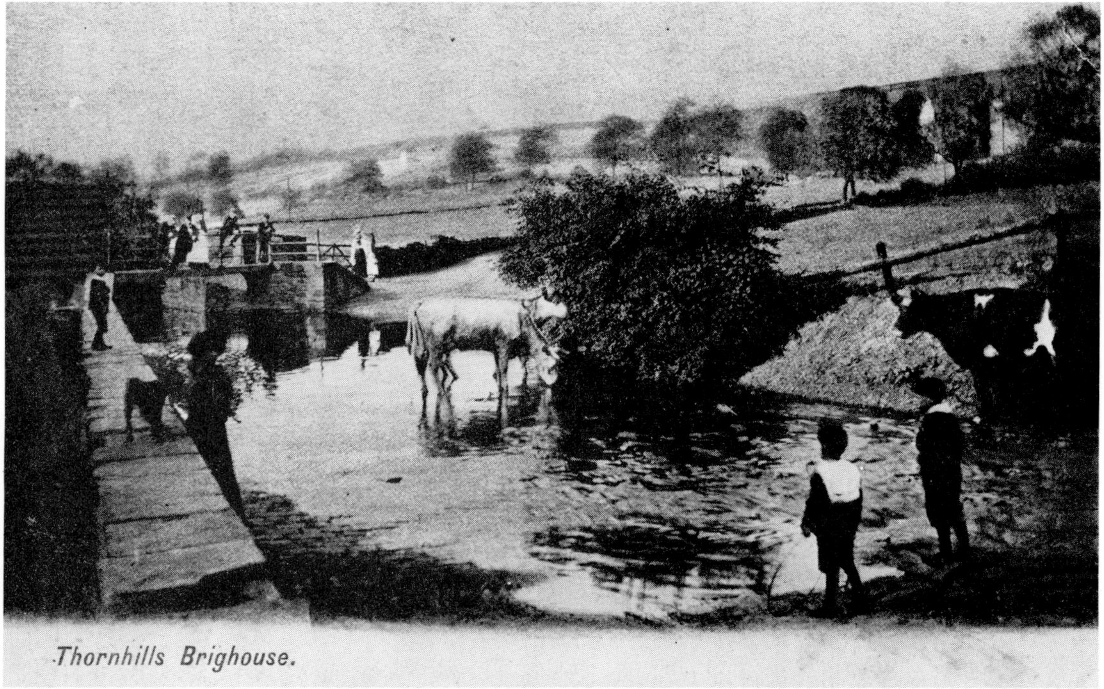

52. *Thornhill Briggs.* Leaving Bailiffe Bridge behind and continuing towards Brighouse along Bradford Road, we next enter the area called Thornhill Briggs. In 1905 Sir George Armitage proposed to the Brighouse Council that a footbridge should be provided at Thornhill Briggs, to aid workers to cross Clifton Beck at that point, instead of having either to wade across or go round via Brighouse. During the heated debate that followed Councillor Fell retorted that 'the bridges cost would be very modest, because I could p..s halfway across the beck at that point'. The chairman ruled Councillor Fell was out of order and Fell replied: 'If I had been in order, I could have reached the other side of the beck.' The picture postcard shows the bridge that was finally built, the ford alongside and a number of children that always seem to be attracted to water. One young man seems to be holding a bowling-hoop, that used to be a favourite pastime.

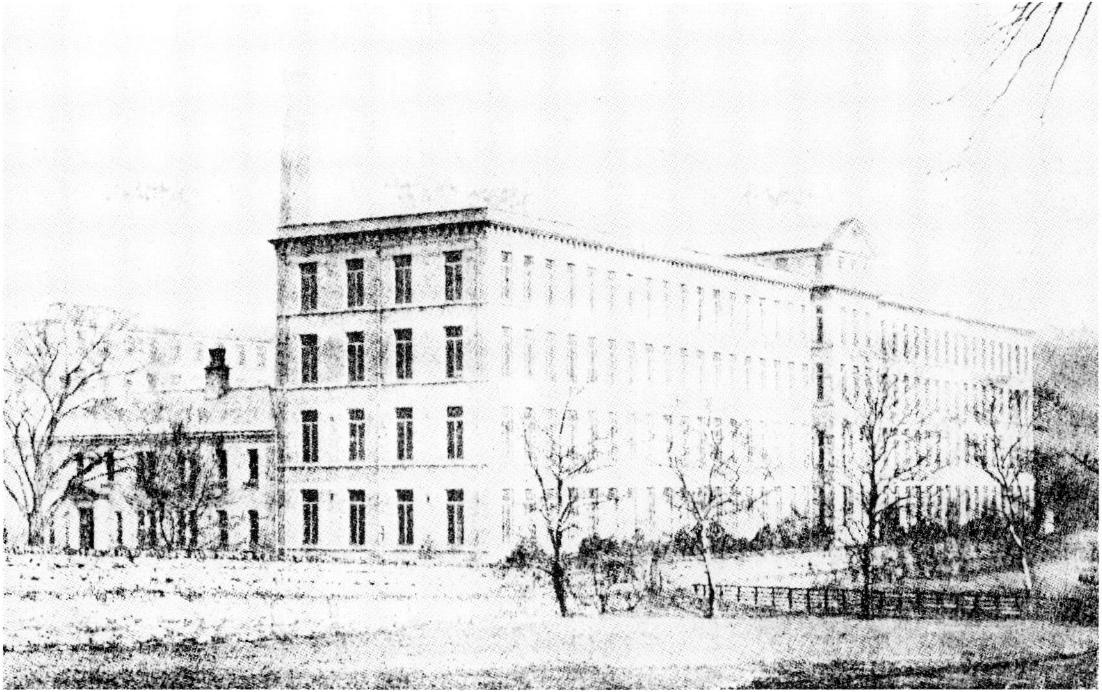

53. *Woodvale Mills.* To the Brighouse side of the ford, towards the end of 1880 you would have seen a new mill being built, for Robert Kershaw. Woodvale Mills was built specifically because of the growing silk trade and for the vast production of silk materials, at that time. Its architect was George Hepworth and the area covered by this magnificent structure was a full five acres. At its height of production it had 40,000 spindles operating on the premises. The silk trade dwindled and in 1904 Ormerod Brothers bought the business and later converted it to synthetic yarns. Later still some parts were split down into smaller units until they became vacant and disused. In 1985 the whole mill became ravaged by fire, in a spate of fires around the Brighouse area and the following year it was demolished.

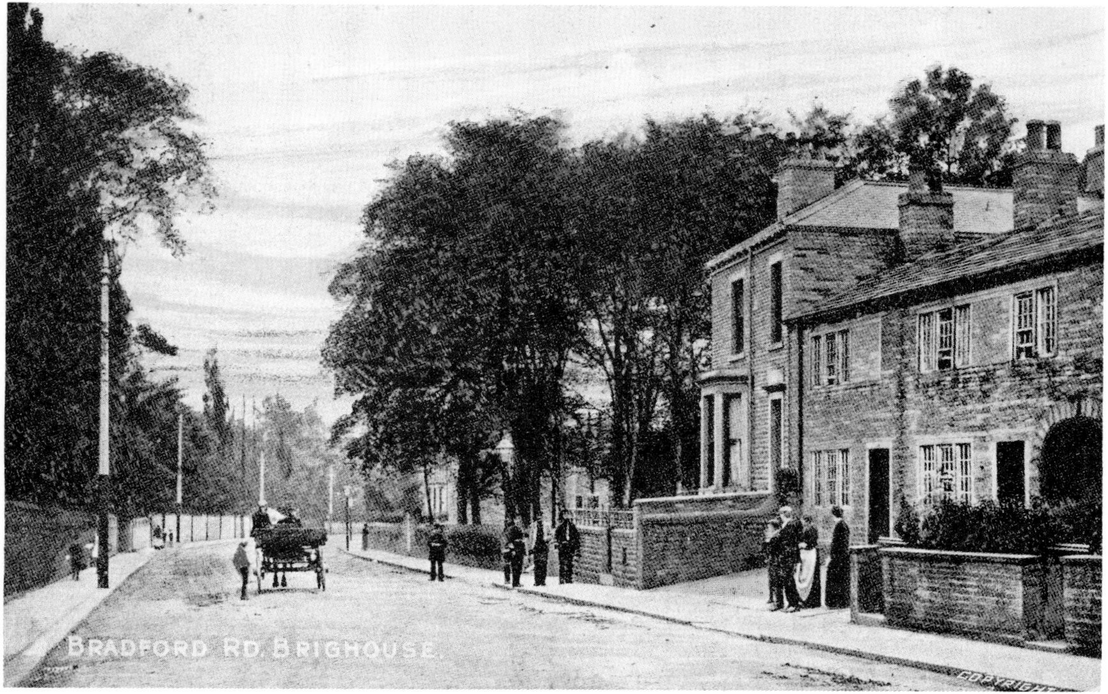

54. Rookery Place. Nearly back to Brighouse centre again, in fact St. James' Church would have been just out of sight around the bend in Bradford Road, when the above card was printed. To the left hand side of the road, just beyond the first post can be seen the entrance to Well Holme, in the estate of Camm Park, and the home of the Camm family for quite a number of years. This became Wellholme Park. On the right hand side, the larger of the buildings is Kingston House, still there to-day, as are the little cottages; said to be the oldest in the district, although they are now one house. Beneath the stone-floored cellar of one of the cottages is a well which has a drop, to the water therein, of forty feet. Passed these buildings, where the trees are in the picture, is now Rookery Place which took its name from the hundreds of rooks that used to nest in those trees.

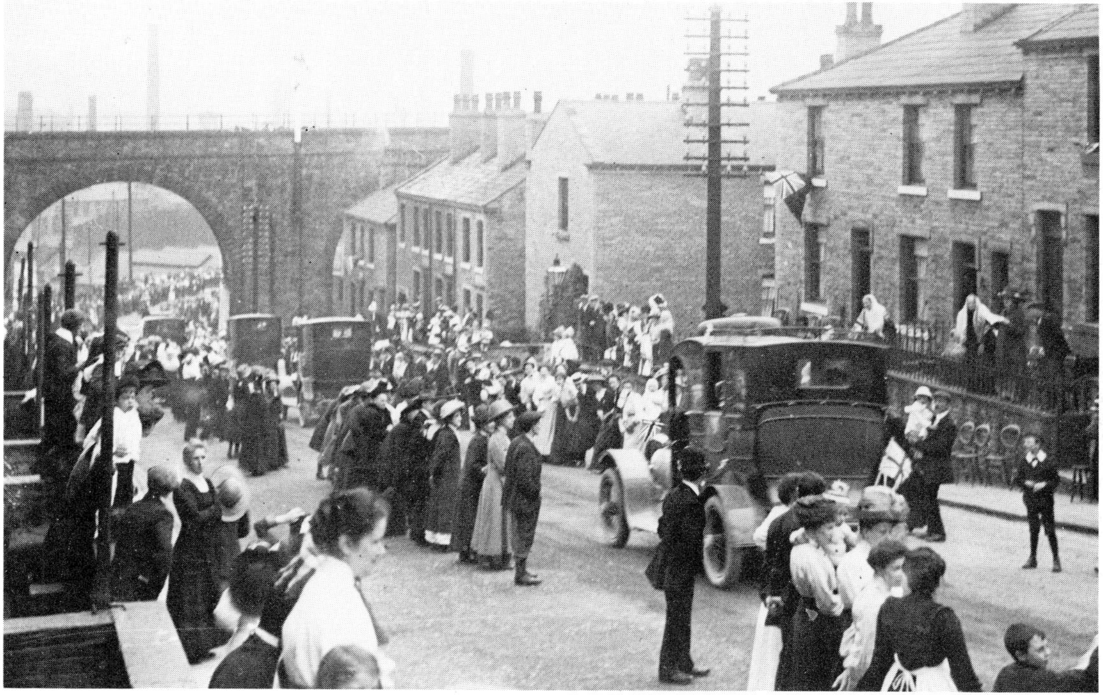

55. *Royal Visit.* Passing Brighouse by and leaving from the junction of King Street and Police Street, we come to the bottom of Clifton Common. During a coronation celebration tour King George V and Queen Mary , on 10th July 1912, drove slowly from Cleckheaton through Clifton village and down Clifton Common, on its way along Police Street and Huddersfield Road to the Brighouse Railway Station. The Echo wrote of the King: *Not tall, nor of commanding presence, scarcely regal from the point of view of stature. A neatly dressed, somewhat dapper, thoroughly gentlemanly man.* The tour had stayed away from all the large towns and cities, to meet the 'ordinary' people, but it was regretted that the carriage had not been an open-topped one. An incident when Lady Armitages car was stopped by a zealous policeman, was soon solved when the lady produced her passcard. The railway bridge shown in the picture has since been taken down.

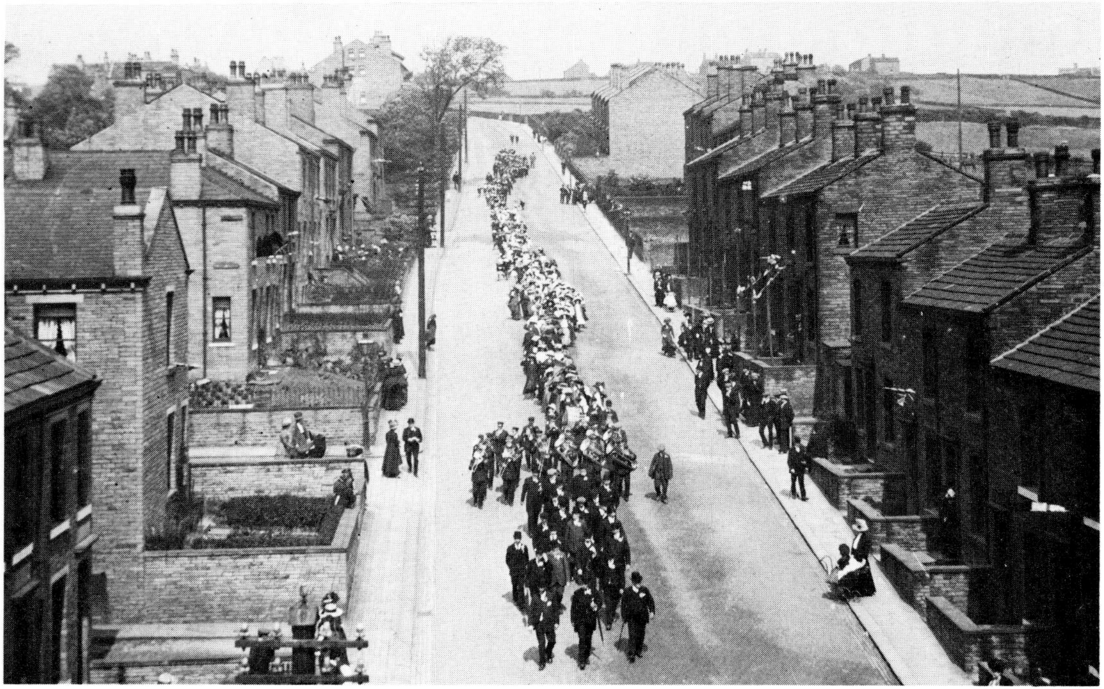

56. *Coronation Procession.* On 7th April 1911, a coronation committee was formed at Clifton, with G. Turver as its chairman, to organise a celebration of the coronation of King George V and Queen Mary. Sir George Armitage was asked to head the subscription list, that was to provide 800 children under fourteen years old, with a party and coronation mugs. The children of the village were told to assemble at their schools where they were marshalled into a procession which at 2 o'clock marched to Westgate. Then, led by organisers and the Clifton Brass Band, they paraded down Clifton Common to Alegar Street, returning to the village green via the same route. Hymns were sung at various stages of the journey and on arrival at the green, the coronation mugs were presented. Buns and coffee were then served at the schools and later entertainment, in the form of sports and games for young and old, was held in the cricket field behind the Armytage Arms public house.

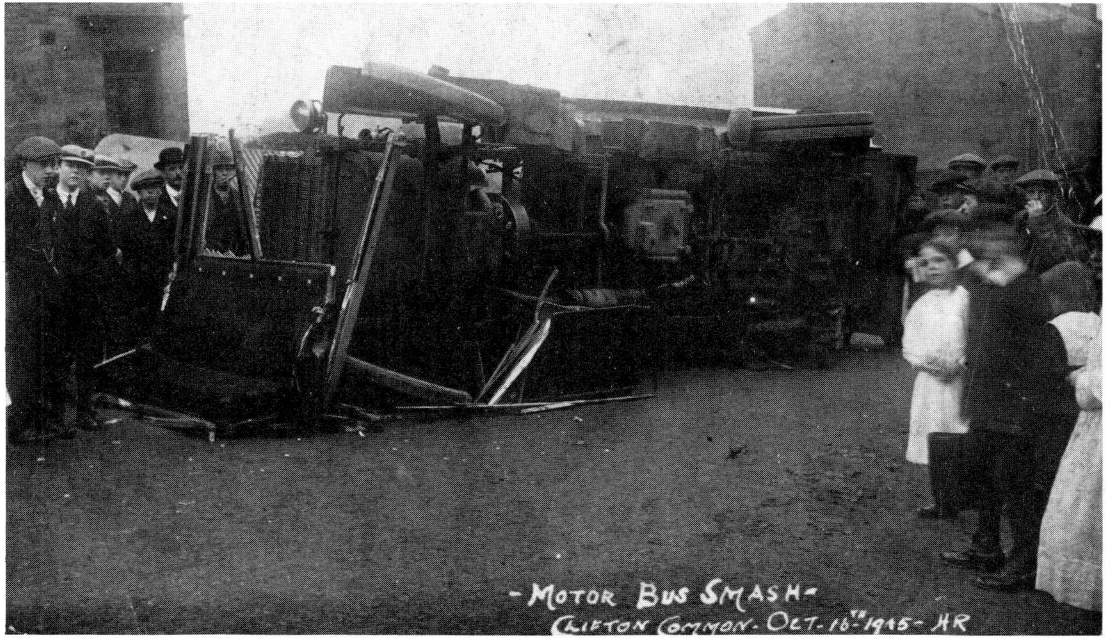

57. *Motor Bus Smash.* The Brighouse Echos account of the above accident, records that the Yorkshire Electric Tramway Co. Ltds. bus from Morley to Brighouse, had about thirty passengers on board, some waiting to alight as it came to the Armytage Arms bus stop. The bus driver, John Clerk, tried the brakes, but nothing happened and the bus carried on over the brow, and began to descend Clifton Common. The conductor, Benjamin Holmes, jumped off the bus and grabbing an iron bar, tried to block the wheels. This failed, however, and the driver stayed at his post, fighting the steering wheel as the vehicle picked up speed. The back wheel came off just before Gin Pit Hill, and the bus hit a telegraph pole and overturned throwing everyone into disarray. Before this happened, Mr. W.H. Smith of Clifton leaped off, falling into the road with tremendous force, dying almost instantly from his injuries. The wheel weighing 5cwt. rolled on down the road; knocked Laura Jagger over, breaking her leg, as she was walking with Ada Pratt; rolled on through the railway arch, smashed open a boundry wall and ended in a croft adjoining Robin Hood Mill. Over twenty people were injured and three died in this awful accident.

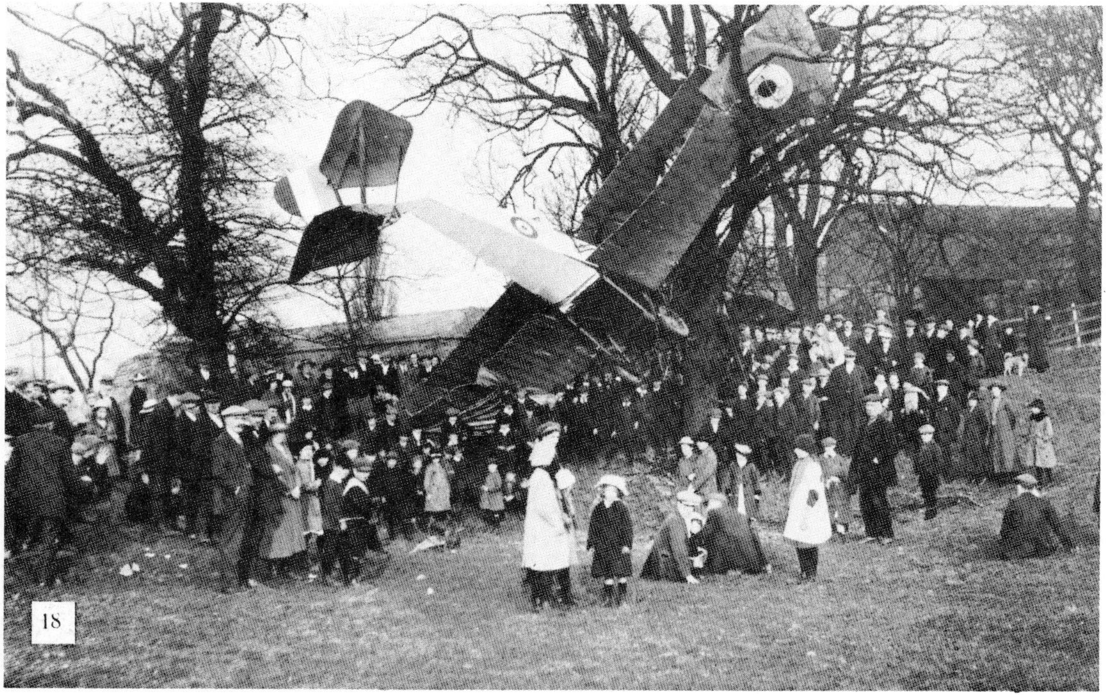

58. *Herbert Sykes.* To a large field along Highmoor Lane, behind the Armytage Arms, in 1920, a gentleman named Mr. Herbert Sykes O.B.E., a renowned Clifton airman, brought his bi-plane in order to take some of the local inhabitants for their first flight in an aircraft. Brighouse had had an earlier introduction to flying, thanks to Herbert, who having obtained his licence in 1915, used to practise around the district. He became a flying instructor during the First World War and after used to organise flying weeks at the Gun Club Field at Lightcliffe. In 1920 the Gun Club Field was not available, so in that year he returned to the field at Clifton. Seventy people took a trip in the new Avro machine, including Brigadier R.E. Sugden, his daughter and an old lady from Mansfield, Mrs. Ann Sissons, aged 101 years. Mr. Sykes named his aircraft 'Psyche' which was a play on words between his own name and that of the classical goddess of beauty.

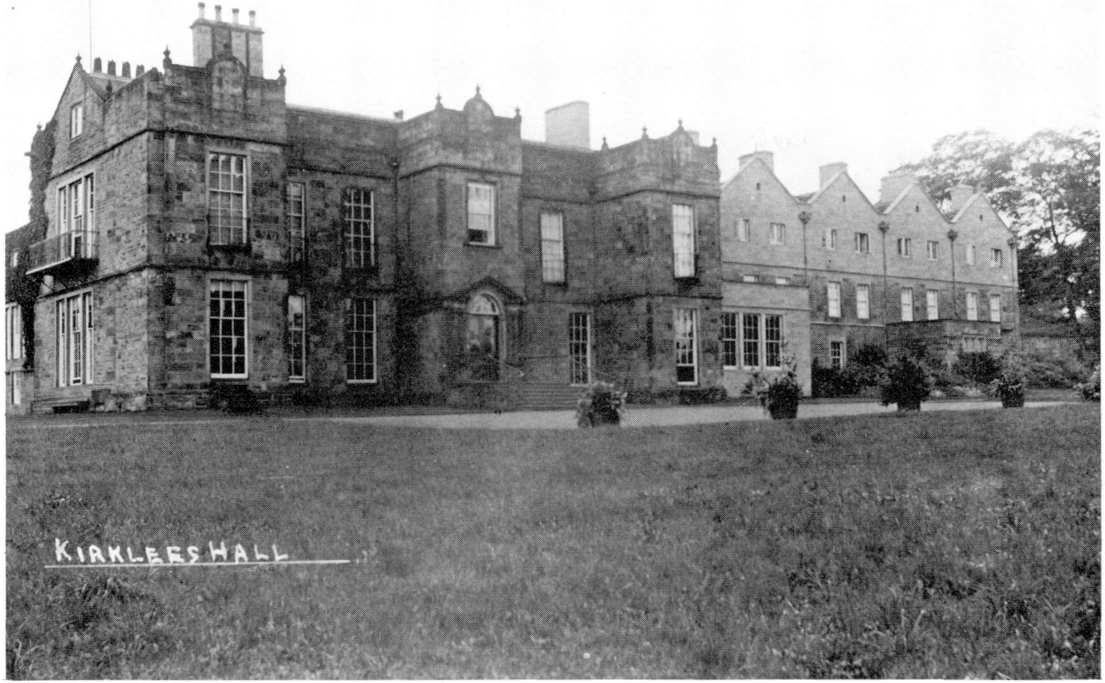

59. *Kirklees Hall.* The Kirklees area, that is the district covered by the old Huddersfield Borough Council, takes its name from Kirklees Hall in Clifton, but Clifton used to be covered by the Brighouse Council. Around 1100 the manor of Clifton came into the possession of the Le Fleming family and Raynor Le Fleming founded the Cistercial Nunnery at Kirklees about 1155, a charter that was confirmed by King Henry III. Later Kirklees lands were granted to Tasburgh and Saville in 1544, but by 1565 they were being acquired by John Armitage of Farnley Tyas, a clothier. John died in a ship wreck in the Irish Sea, but the land stayed with the family. The part of the hall which is now the west wing, was built, using stone from part of the old priory, around 1565, as a house. The present hall was built in 1610 and extensions have been added since then. The building was immortalised by Charlotte Bronte in her book 'Shirley', when she used it as a model for Nunwood. She stayed here on a number of occasions.

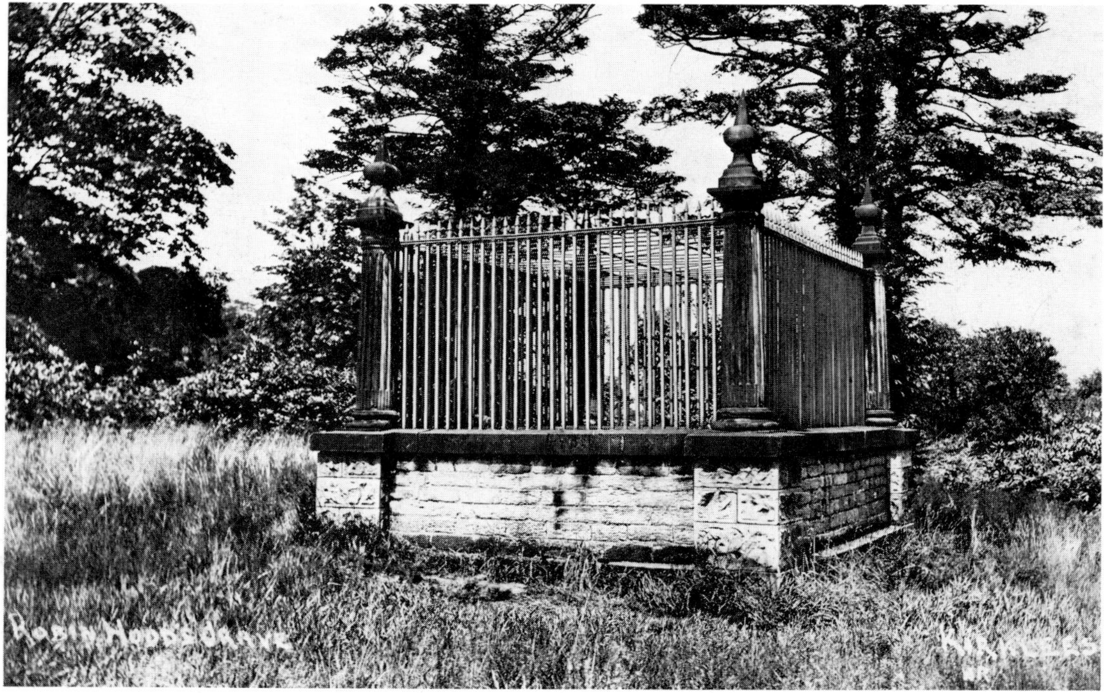

60. *Robin Hoods Grave.* In the early part of the twentieth century visitors to the area could take a guided tour of the Kirklees Estate. As T. Mitcheson wrote in 1917: *We then passed the front of the hall with its many gabled front of differing kinds of architecture from, we were told, the twelfth to the seventeenth or eighteenth century... Thence we were led on a path to Robin Hoods Grave, which is railed off and protected from spoilation and noticed the inscription.* The inscription on the stone reads in translation: 'Here underneath this little stone, lies Robert, Earl of Huntington. Never archer were, as he, so good. And people called him Robin Hood. Such outlaws as he and his men, will England never see again. Dated 24th. December 1247.' The estate is now closed to visitors, and the last report was that the grave was broken down and in need of repair.

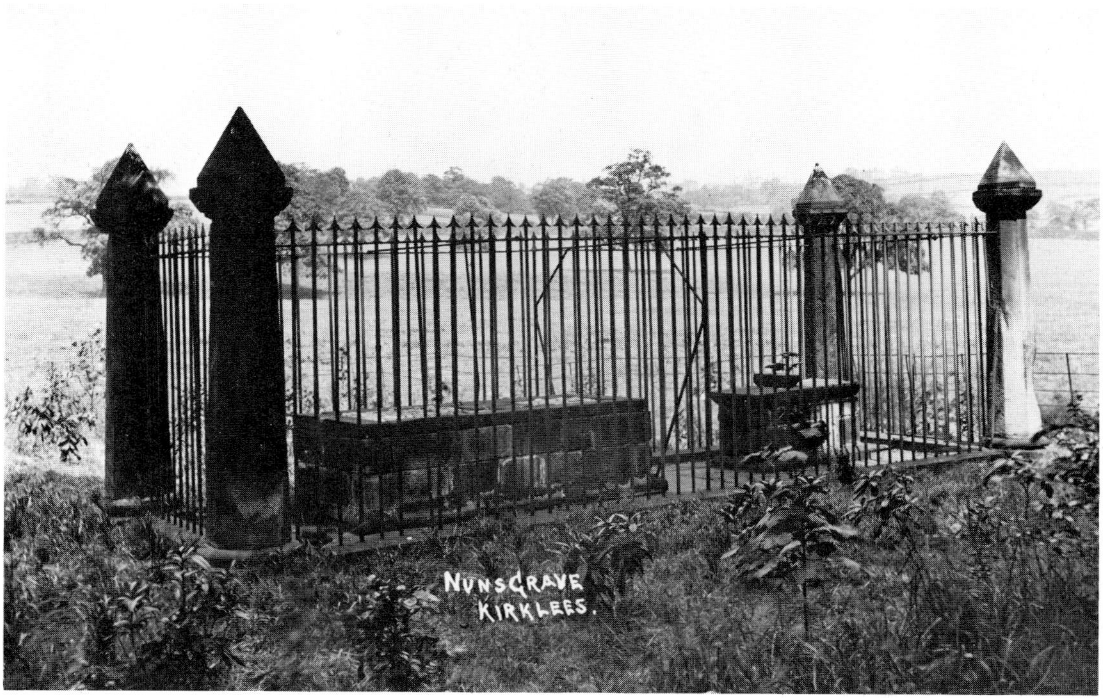

61. *Nuns Grave.* The above postcard shows the grave of the first prioress, on record, of Kirklees Priory; her name was Elizabeth de Staynton. The Norman-French inscription that was once readable on her tombstone when translated reads: 'Sweet Jesus of Nazareth, son of God, have mercy on Elizabeth Stainton, Prioress of this house.' Robin Hood, so the story goes, came to see this lady of the cloth, in the year 1247, at the ripe old age of eighty-seven, to be 'blooded' from his pains. Now whether from vengance or through a mistake the prioress bled him to such a degree that he barely had the strength to blow his horn and summon his friend John Little. From his death-bed, aided by John, he shot an arrow from one of the upper rooms of the priory and where it landed, there he was buried.

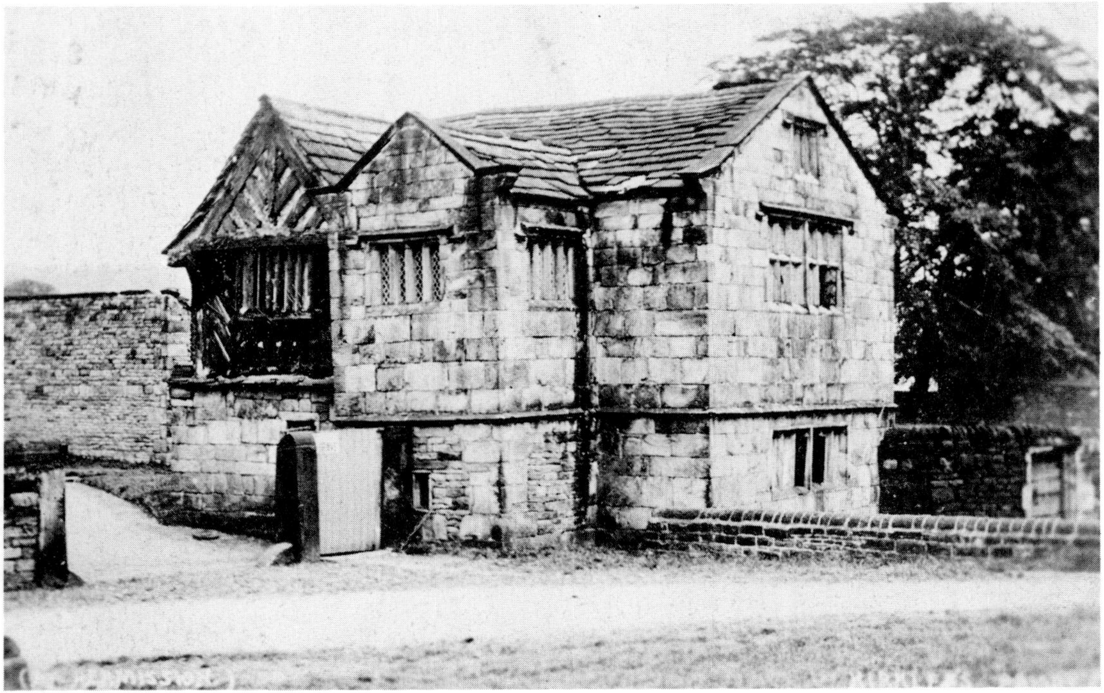

62. *Kirklees Priory*. The gatehouse of the old Priory is the only part of the building still standing, with its ancient black and white timbers. The 'Nonnes' of Karkales' as the founders deed puts it, were Cistercian Nuns and each wore a white tunic or robe, a black scapular or headdress and a girdle. Our friend Mr. T. Mitcheson on his visit states: *From here we were directed down to the remains of the Abbey or Nunnery where we saw the tombstone of Elizabeth de Stayton, the princess who is supposed to have been Robin Hoods' 'cousin', she lies with other prioresses at the east end of the Priory Church. We were shown the chamber from which Robin Hood, with the aid of John Little, shot his arrow. Sir George Armitage has had carefully marked out the lines of the church and nunnery as they originally stood.*

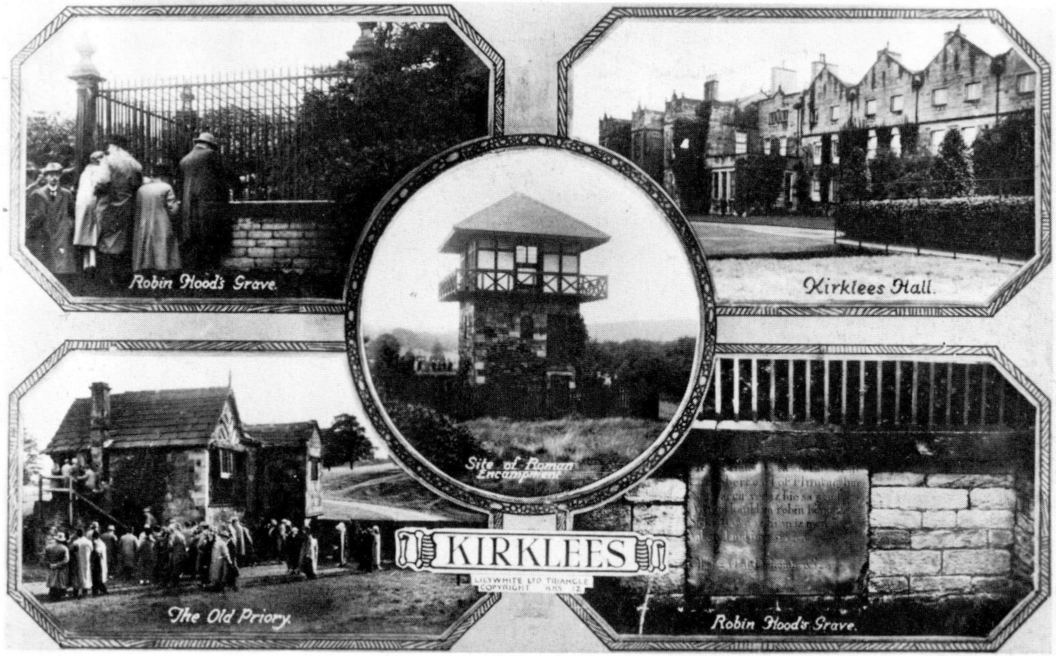

63. *Roman Encampment (centre)*. T. Mitcheson goes on to tell us that: *From there we soon had a view of the Roman tower, a new erection, faithful in type of an original which is a look-out station at the point of intersection of the old roman roads crossing the camp. This camp was bored by Sir George a few years ago, and he on carefully covering up the old walls, had placed on the surface, stones to indicate its size and shape for future visitors.* A main road ran from Chester to Manchester, thence to Slack; between Huddersfield and Nonts Sarahs, then into and passed this encampment at Kirklees, on to Filey or Filey Bay, and thus if a line is drawn on a map, from say, Filey to Chester, it will touch or pass through all of the forgoing places.

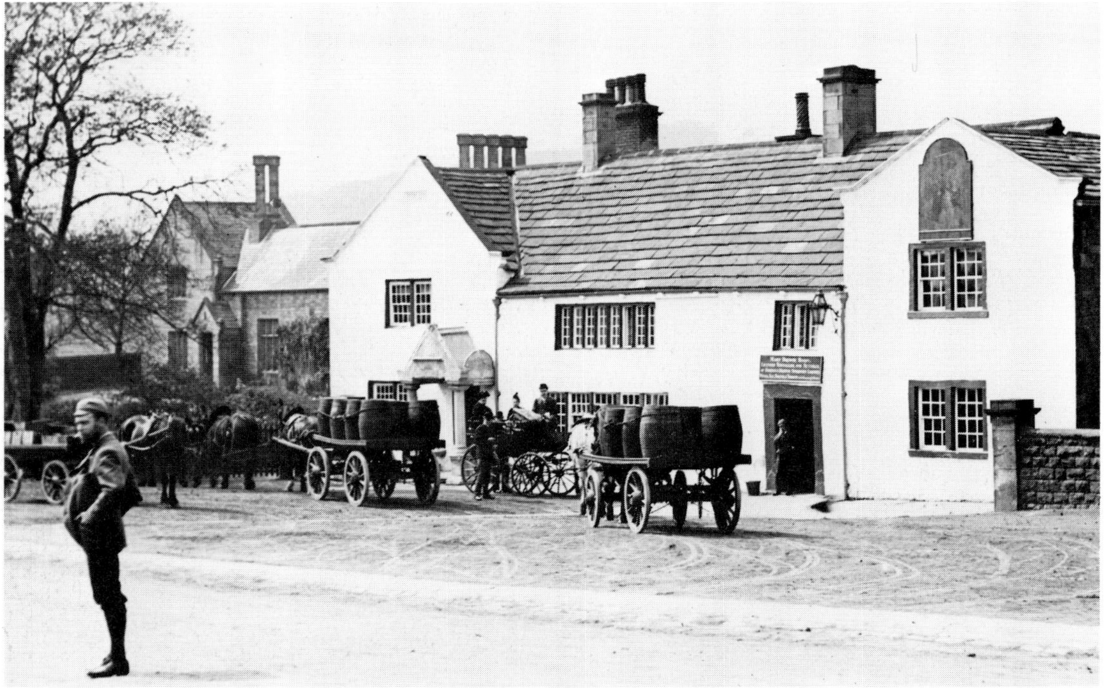

64. *Three Nuns.* Yet another building associated with the Bronte family, The Three Nuns, an historic inn that stood on the crossroads of Wakefield Road and Leeds Road. In Mrs. Gaskells 'Life of Charlotte Bronte', the inn is mentioned as a place where 'fustion-dressed mill-hands' gathered. Mrs. Gaskell suggests that it once was an old manor house and it certainly looks more like one than a public house. In 1812 it is said to have been a Luddite meeting place – they met in a nearby field on the night of the attack on Rawfolds Mill. Around 1920 the ceiling in one of the rooms fell in and uncovered knives and swords believed to have been Luddite relics. No-one knows exactly when it was built, but it was pulled down to make room for a newer public house in the 1930s.

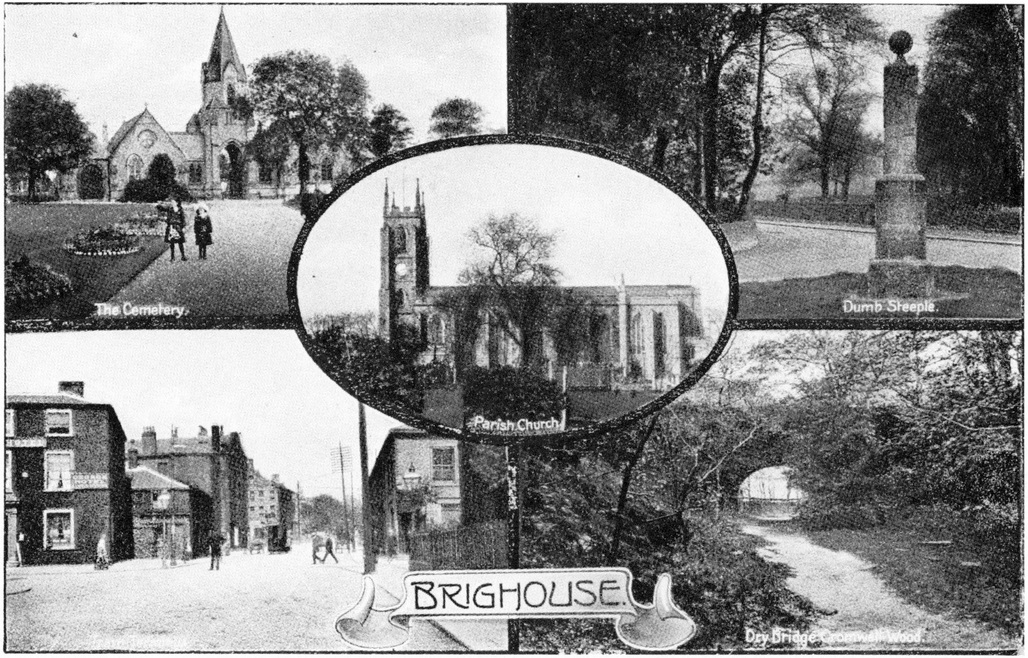

65. *Dumb Steeple.* Not far from the Three Nuns in the middle of the Leeds-Wakefield crossroads stood the 'Dumb Steeple', a solid piece of stone, some twenty-six feet high, looking like an old church belfry, but with no opening for either bell or bellringer. Its reverse silence has obtained it its name, but could also have been a corruption of 'Doomed Steeple'. A guilty person fleeing from the law was able to claim sanctuary at this obelisk and anyone who was following was doomed to failure. It may have been a sanctuary cross, although it has never been mentioned anywhere about the priory of Kirklees, not so far away. The steeple is mentioned in Mrs. G. Linnaeus Banks 'In Bondage', about the Luddite revolt. It has now been replaced, in the middle of the road, by a roundabout, and installed at the side of the road.

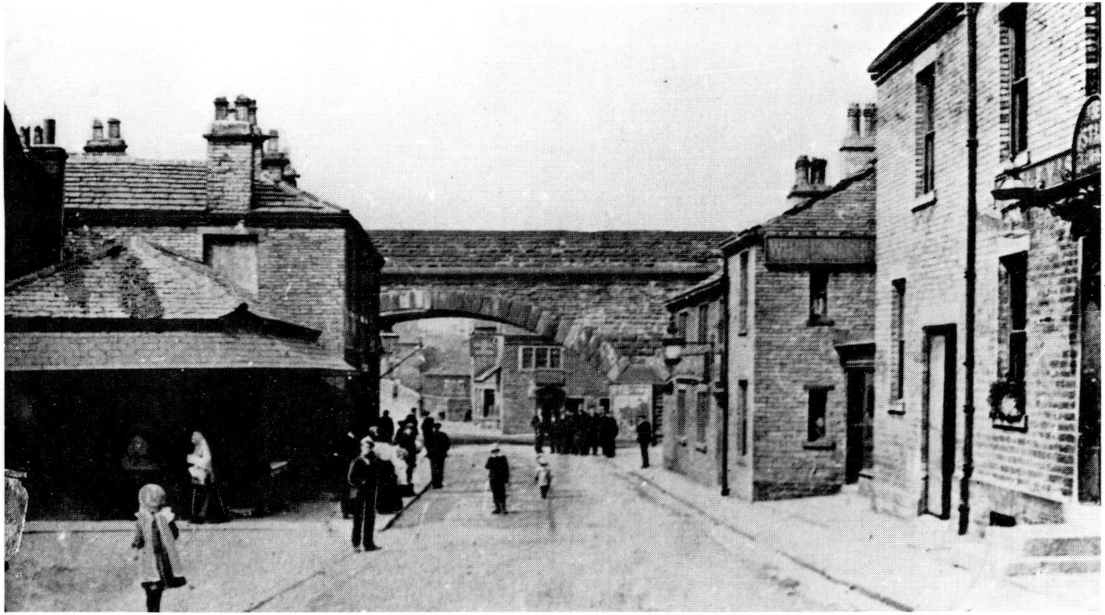

66. *Bridge End.* Over on the other side of Brighouse, out past Briggate, we move into a section of Bridge End that must have been a drinkers paradise in the earlier part of this century. In this part of the town there were four public houses within a very short distance. You will be able to see three of these in the postcard above. If you look through the railway bridge, you will see the sign for The Duke of York Inn; on this side of the bridge and on the same side of the road is The White Lion and just in the picture on the extreme right is The Star. The Star is the only one of the taverns left still standing. A small car park has taken the place of the Duke of York Inn, built up waste ground is where the White Lion was and the fourth pub, The Rising Sun, would have been where the road to the left is, only it had already been pulled down.

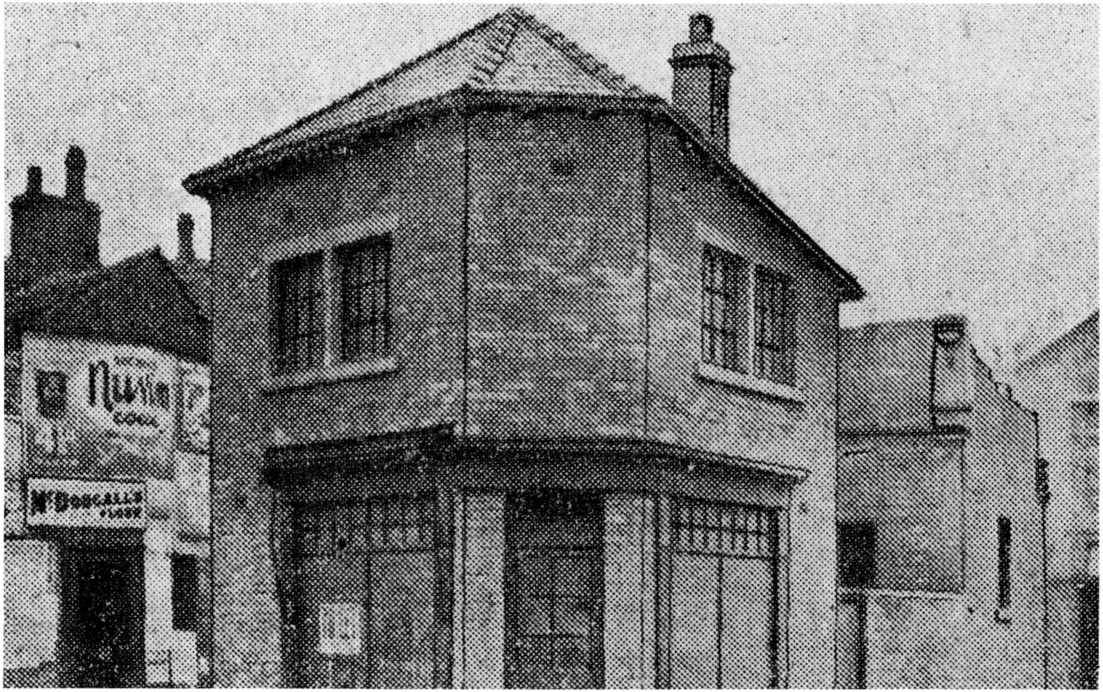

67. *The Rising Sun.* As you may probably have noticed from the number of scenes in this book, which include a tavern or an inn, Brighouse was a well-known place for drinking and for its drunkards. This is the fourth of the public houses that made up the drinkers paradise, at Bridge End. As can be seen, it stood right in the middle of the entrance to Bramston Street, now the main road to Rastrick. Around the turn of the century, however, the Magistrates Court began to clamp down on the drinkers and on the number of public houses, where people could do their 'secret drinking'. The Rising Sun became one of the pubs that had to go, the last licensee being H. Womersley, who took over in August 1905. This photograph was taken in July-August 1913, shortly before it was demolished in a road widening scheme. In the left hand side of the picture is the corner shop, with advertisements for McDougalls flour and selling cocoa at 4½d.

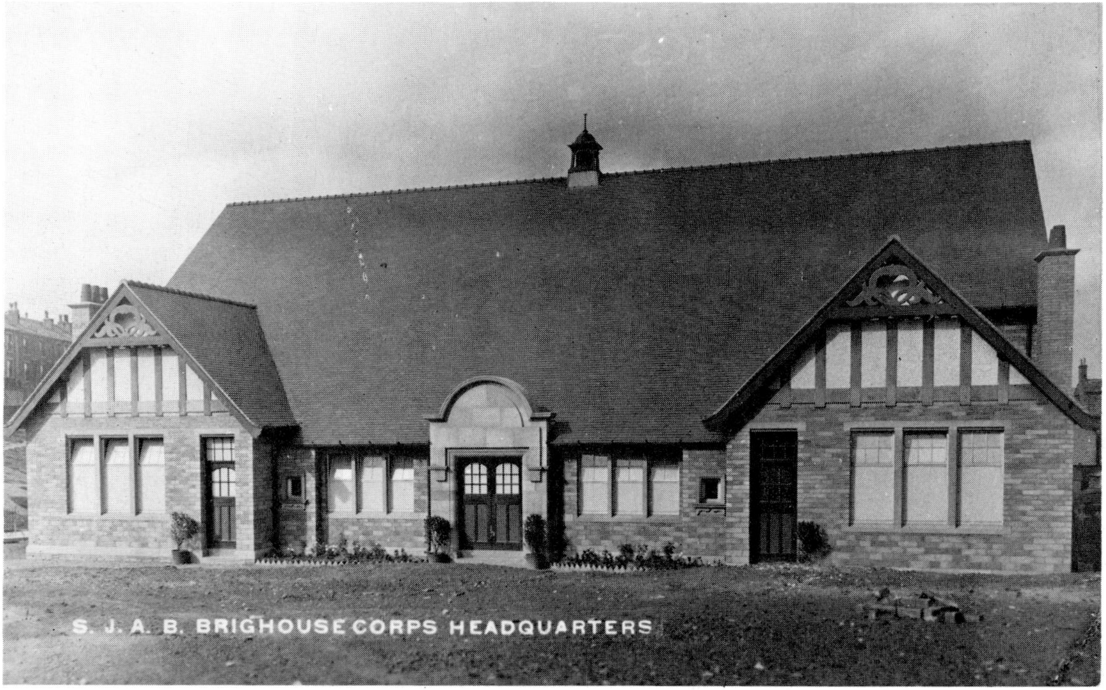

68. *St. John's Ambulance.* Heading up Bramston Street, on the left hand side, before the playing fields, we come to the above building. A branch of the St. John's Ambulance Society was established in Brighouse in 1882, and provided a one horse ambulance to deal with any casualties. The vehicle was a rather ramshackled affair and something better was soon needed. In 1899 a Grand Ball to raise money for a 'thoroughly equipped horse ambulance' was held in the Town Hall. A very enthusiastic ambulance brigade was soon formed and by 1911 they had decided that they needed a headquarters and started to organise fund-raisers to help pay for its erection. A bazaar raised £540 in only four days, so the building fund was off to a great start. In 1912 the above site became available and a year later the foundation stone was laid. With the formation of the National Ambulance Brigade the building was too large for its usage and was eventually sold to become a chapel of rest.

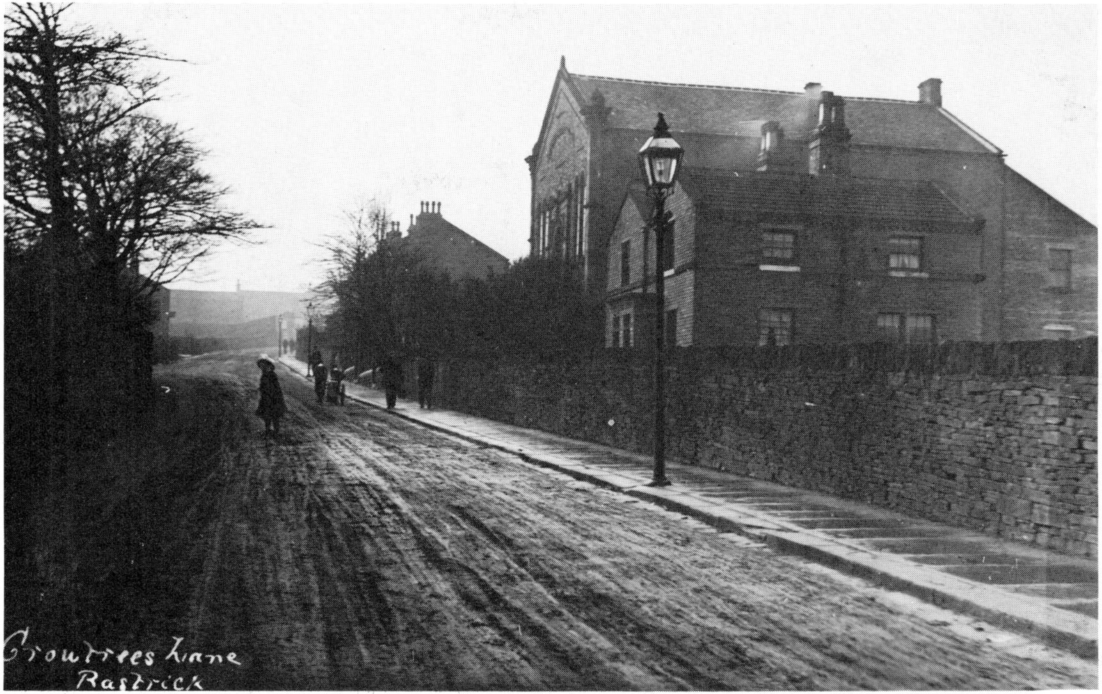

69. *Crowtrees Lane.* Continuing up into Rastrick, after the 'top oft town', we enter Crowtrees Lane, this scene being around 1912. At that time, the small roadway, that is to right hand side as we go up, was the original Crowtrees Lane, and didn't it look bleak. There are no houses down the left side of the lane, in the picture, that we would see to-day, but there is the old Crowtrees Chapel that later in its history, amalgamated with the new St. Matthew's Church and in the early 1960s was demolished. When it was finally decided that the tramway lines from Huddersfield were to be laid around through Rastrick, a new road was put down, to the right of this picture, leaving this lane as a quiet driveway for the housing that had been built to the left.

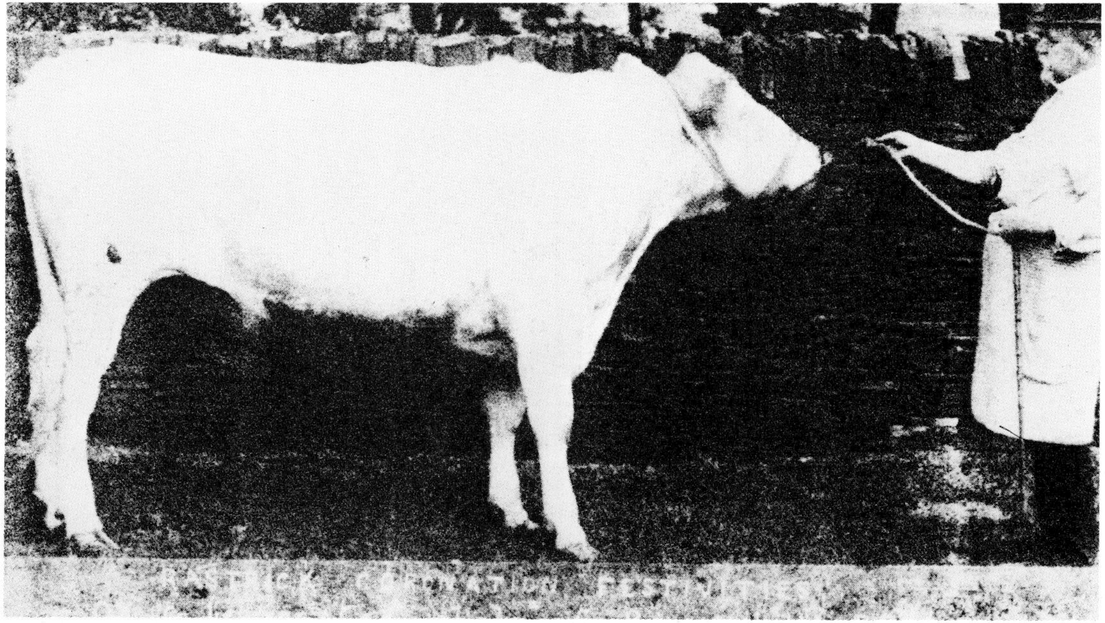

70. *Ox Roast.* The coronation of King George V in 1911 was celebrated, not only at Clifton and Brighouse, but also at Round Hill, Rastrick. The Rastrick arrangements, in addition to a procession of the school children with songs, sports and a bonfire, at Round Hill, included a separate committee who were to try their hand at an ox roast, a house to house collection helping to defray the cost. A bullock was purchased by Mortons butchers, Church Street, from the Leeds cattle market and arrived on 13th June, weighing in at 13cwt., and was processed through the streets to the stable at Thornton Arms public house. The oven to roast the ox was made of 4,000 bricks and insulated to keep the heat in. 2,000 tickets for the event were distributed and 120 yard loaves, weighing ½ st. each were ordered. The meat was done to a turn and over 3,000 sandwiches were consumed, as hawkers of havercakes, soaked in ox fat, called 'penny dips' strolled the field. The schools of the district were given a weeks holiday, as an extra celebration.

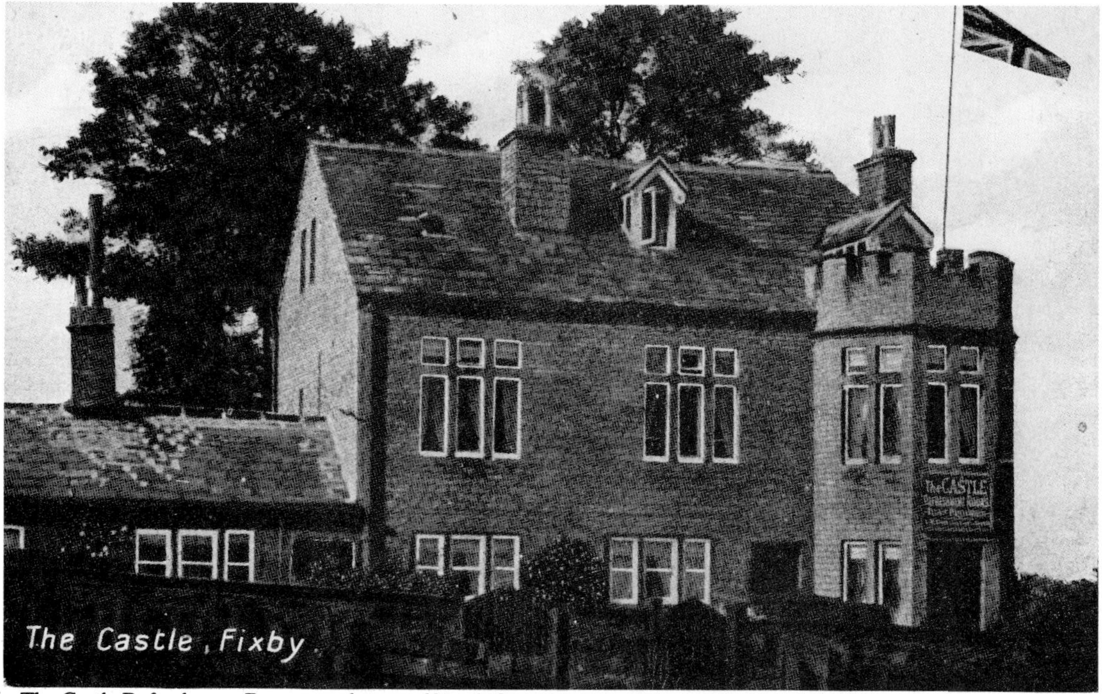

71. ***The Castle.*** **The Castle Refreshment Rooms, at the top of North Cross Lane, in Fixby, used to be owned in** 1905 by Mr. C.W. Sharp. After a nice week-end ramble past Fixby Hall, and through the woods, you could call at the Castle for tea and scones and if the weather was fair, sit in the large greenhouse at the rear of the house, while refreshing yourself for the return journey. This house was situated at the boundary with Fartown, Huddersfield and the nearest wall in the above scene was the boundary wall. At one time the turret at the end of the house used to be six feet higher, but was lowered, so that a dorma-window could be installed, as above, circa 1903. Sadly the tea rooms are no longer in fruition, but the house still stands, minus the little cottages to the left, which have been replaced by a garage. The roof of the house now has modern tiles on it, the centre dorma is twice its size and the dorma over the turret has gone, with the flag-pole. Fixby now comes under the care of the Kirklees (Huddersfield) Council.

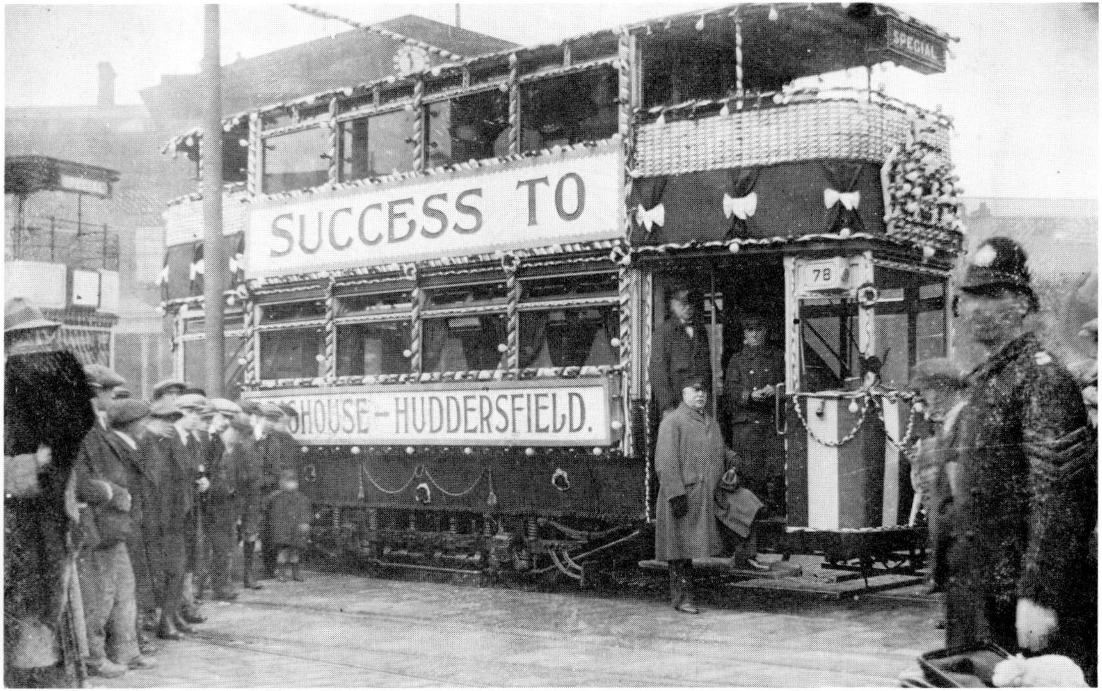

72. *First Tram (1).* As early as 1899 there was talk of a tramway system in Brighouse, the line to run from town, through Hove Edge, Hipperholme, Lightcliffe Bailiffe Bridge and back to Brighouse. In the same year Halifax offered to bring trams to Brighouse and negotiations had begun, with Huddersfield, to bring a line through Rastrick, to 'George Corner'. Both Huddersfield and Halifax put bills to parliament, but only Halifax was successful. A little later Huddersfield sought parliamentary powers to bring a line through Ash Brow to Brighouse, but not via Rastrick. This was strongly opposed by Brighouse Council and in 1914 both parties signed an agreement to bring trams around through Rastrick. The outbreak of the First World War soon put the project even further back. Halifax trams had long ago reached the town, including the short line from Bailiffe Bridge. Eventually in 1923 the Huddersfield-Brighouse tramway was opened.

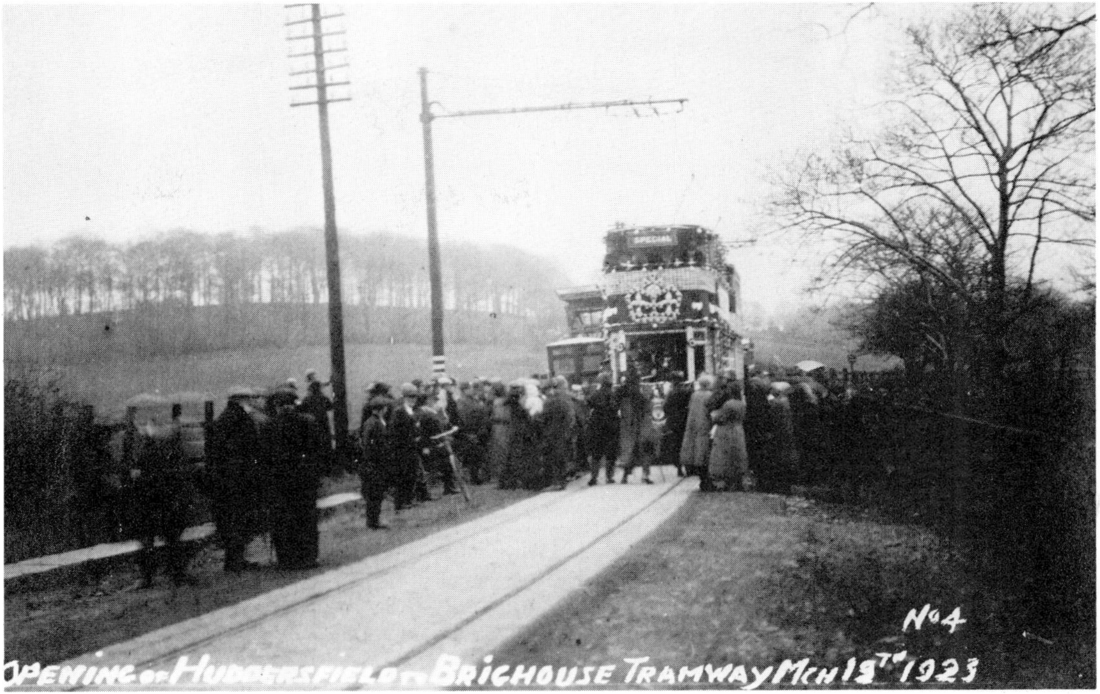

73. *First Tram (2).* On 12th March 1923 a beautifully decorated tram-car left Huddersfield, Georges Square at 11.30 a.m. and arrived at the Fixby boundary where it stopped to pick up the Mayor and Mayoress of Brighouse, Alderman and Mrs. G.F. Sugden, who had been transported there by coach. On board already were the Mayor and Mayoress of Huddersfield and quite a number of the Huddersfield Council. The tram was driven from Fixby to Brighouse by G.F. Sugden and on the return journey Mrs. Dawson, the Huddersfield Mayoress, collected the fares. Forty of the old people of Brighouse were transported for free on this journey – their combined ages totalling 2,994 years, an average age of 73. Had the project of the Huddersfield-Brighouse tramway been completed in 1914, it would have cost £48,000, instead of the £81,000 it did cost.

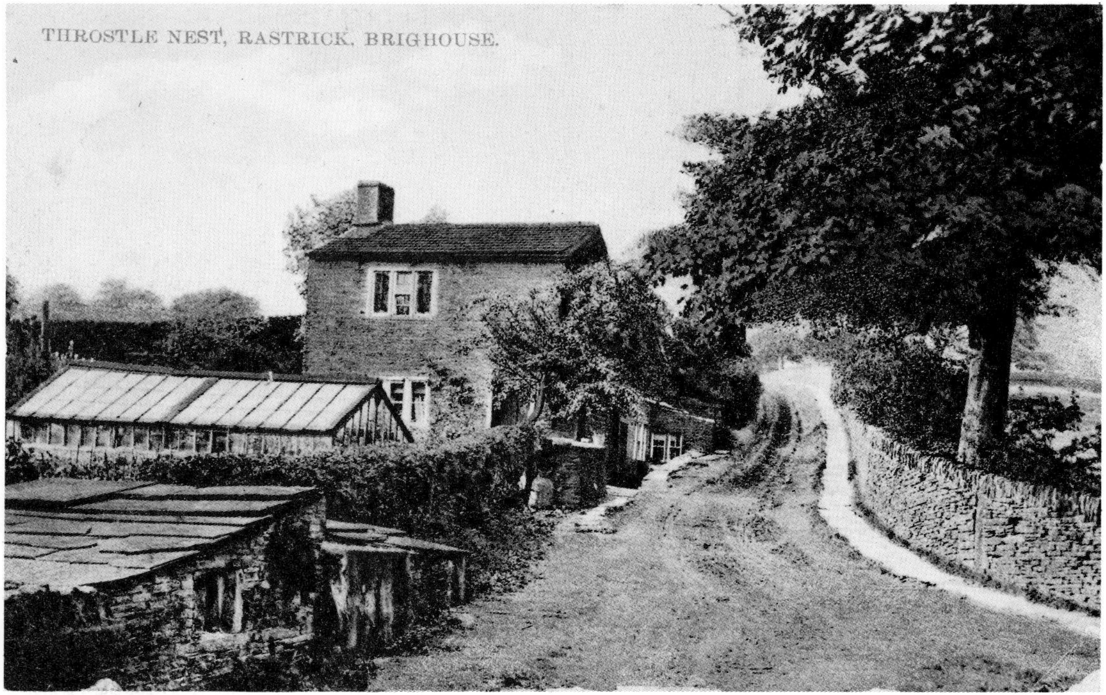

74. *Throstle Nest.* Just a short distance from the M62 and to the left, as we reach the top of Huddersfield Road, is Bradley Woods. Throstle Nest Farm was along part of a walk, not far from the Bradley Scout Camp, called Shepherds Thorn Lane. It was a section of Mr. Clement Blackburns Toothill Estate, and when this postcard was published circa 1907, it was lived in by the Walton family. Mr. and Mrs. Joseph Walton and their son Jimmy, were tenant farmers, but Throstle Nest was not so much a farm, more a small-holding where you could buy home-grown tomatos and other produce. Joe Walton, as a side-line, used to make children's toys which were sold through 'Penny Denhams' of Brighouse. Throstle Nest Farm was later purchased by Cornelius Kershaw, a local farmer who passed it on to his son Peter, it became disused between the wars and was eventually demolished.

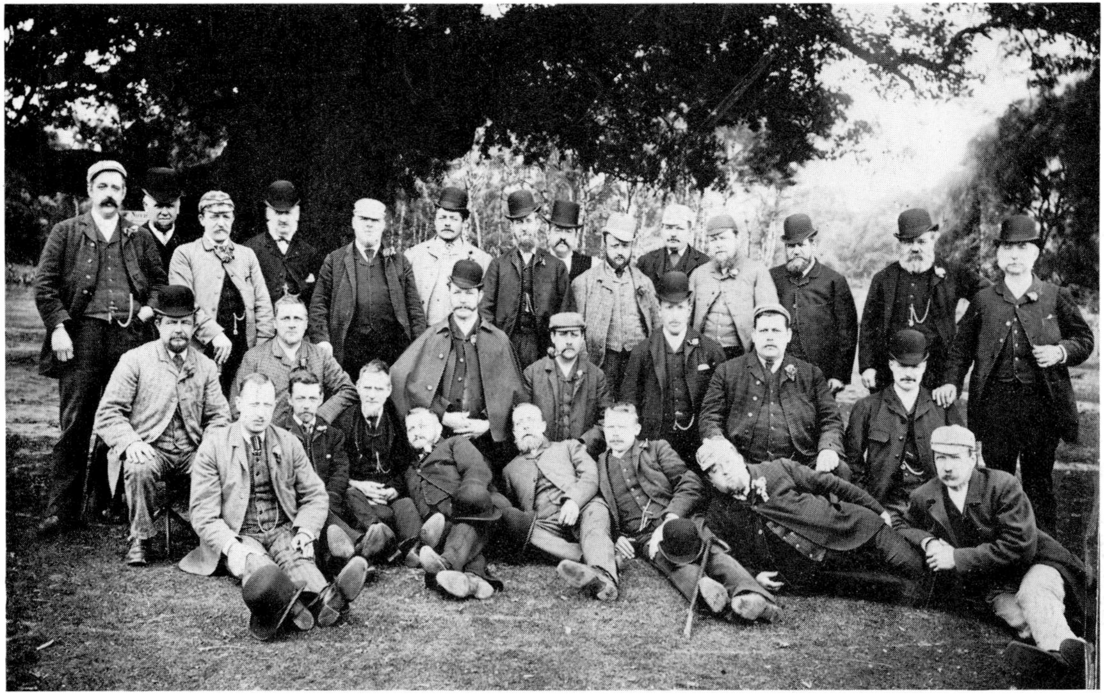

75. *The Henpecked Club.* From around 1895 until about 1914, a rather unusual society was in existence in Brighouse. It was a society for gentlemen who considered that they were not the rulers of their own lives. In other words, they were 'under the thumbs' of their wives. The society was called The Henpecked Club and used to meet at irregular intervals three or four times per year. At these meetings, if anyone had been absent from a previous meeting or were late putting in an appearance, he had to explain his absence or his delay to the rest of the club. Excuses such as 'I could not escape, because the little woman had me chained to the kitchen sink' or 'I hadn't finished darning my socks and ironing my trousers'. Each Easter weekend a day trip to get away from 'the boss', was arranged and the above photograph is thought to be of one of those outings. The society folded with the start of the First World War.

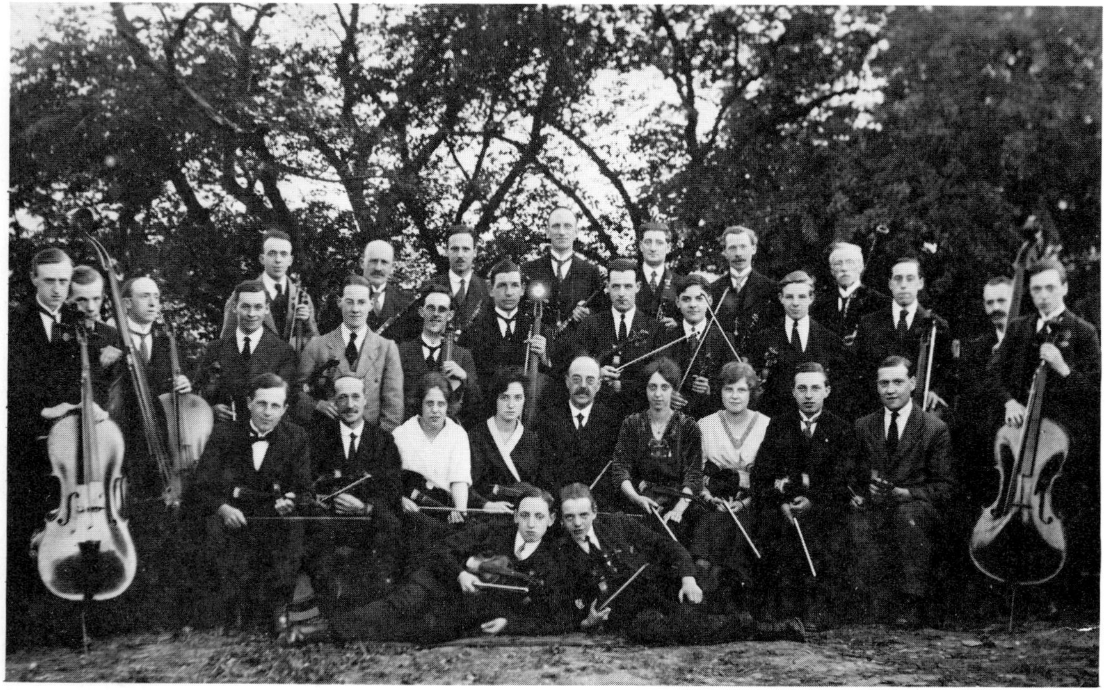

76. *Permanent Orchestra.* **Brighouse has a reputation for producing good brass bands, like the Brighouse** and Rastrick Band, but it has also turned out quite a number of good orchestras. This photograph of the Permanent Orchestra taken about 1919 is one example of this. The members here present are, from left to right, back row: Mr. Hodgson, John Dilley, his son Harry Dilley, who married into Davison coach family, Harry Smith, unknown, Willie Earnshaw and Sam Wood. Middle row: Lorrie Wilkinson, unknown, Vernie Stevens, Walter Lawson, Reggie Mitchell, Frank Sutcliffe, unknown, John Riley, Raymond Woodhouse, Mr. W. Robinson, Willie Forthrop, J.A. Brown on double bass, and unknown. Front row: unknown, Abraham Thorpe, Miss Norah Sheard, Miss Doris Jackson, Hanson Haley who was the orchestra conductor, Miss Nellie Binns, unknown, Mr. Helliwell, and Harry Stake. The two gentlemen at the very front are Wilfred Waddington the lead violin and Sam Shaw. The photograph was taken in a beautiful setting: Sam Woods old hen run.